MARY, THE TEACHER OF JESUS

MONSIGNOR GEORGE TÜTTO

MARY,
the Teacher
of Jesus

ST PAULS

ST PAULS Publishing
Morpeth Terrace, London SW1P 1EP, UK

Copyright (English Translation) © ST PAULS 1999

ISBN 085439 570 9

Set by TuKan, High Wycombe
Produced in the EC
Printed by Interprint Ltd., Marsa, Malta

ST PAULS is an activity of the priests and brothers
of the Society of St Paul who proclaim the Gospel
through the media of social communication

ACKNOWLEDGMENTS

I am most grateful to the following publishers for their permission to quote from their copyright publications:

The scripture quotations are from the *New Jerusalem Bible*, published and copyright 1985 by Darton, Longman & Todd Ltd and les Editions du Cerf, and used by permission of the publishers.

Quotations from Church and Papal Documents, published in English by the Catholic Truth Society, London, are used with permission of the publishers.

Church teaching is quoted from the *Catechism of the Catholic Church*, published in 1994 by Geoffrey Chapman, an imprint of Cassell Plc, London.

Quotations about Arius and Arianism, Nestorius and Monophysitism are taken by permission of Oxford University Press from *The Oxford Dictionary of the Christian Church*, edited by F.L. Cross and E.A. Livingstone, Oxford University Press 1974.

Quotation from *Mary for Today* by Hans Urs von Balthasar, published by St Paul Publications, Slough, 1987, with permission of Johannes Verlag Einsideln, Freiburg.

Permission for the cover picture, *The Holy Family*, work of Sr Angelica Ballan, is given by the Congregation of Sisters Disciples of the Divine Master, Rome.

My special thanks to Sister Monica Gribbin for her invaluable help in correcting my manuscript and in preparing it for publication.

Dedicated
to
His Holiness Pope John Paul II

Contents

Foreword

I am honoured to recommend this work by Mgr George Tütto. I admire his pastoral work, which gives a special dimension to anything he writes. There is an old saying, *Nunquam satis de Maria*, there will never be enough about Mary. Literature about her, abundant before Vatican II, had – after the Council, but not, we hope, due to it – declined. The revival has begun. I am delighted to see Mgr Tütto adding to it.

Let the reader not be surprised at the title. The author shows, by exact quotation, that he is following the lead of Pope John Paul II. He embarks throughout on a path of acute interest, not often taken by writers on Our Lady; it is scarcely necessary to add that he does so with all the delicacy and reverence needed.

As Mgr Tütto makes clear, what the Gospels tell us is basic, essential to our doctrine, upheld by General Councils of the Church and expounded by theologians. But what of the many areas of the life of Christ, of his relations with his Mother and St Joseph, about which the Gospels do not inform us? Here he is stimulating and even provocative, in the good sense of that word.

I applaud the writer's special attention to the Jewish feasts. We have in recent years suddenly become aware of the most obvious thing about Our Lord: his Jewishness. This is a whole world to explore and clarify.

I recommend Mgr Tütto's book to those who presently are seeking a full understanding of the relations between the Sacred Heart of Jesus and the Immaculate Heart of Mary. Pope Jopn Paul II has used an inspiring phrase to describe this mysterious, salvific, sanctifying unity: the Alliance of the two Hearts. Profound, enlightened devotion thus inspired is, happily, spreading worldwide. The Philippines are prominent in promoting it and sound theological research has not been wanting, not without attention to the fruitful intuition of the Jewishness of Jesus and Mary; they are at the summit of the great age of Judaism, centred in the Old Testament teaching on the heart.

I may be permitted to record here a special link between Ireland and Hungary, Mgr Tütto's homeland. In western Hungary in Györ, there is an Irish Madonna. It was brought there in Cromwellian times in my country, by an Irish bishop, Walter Lynch. He was accepted as an auxiliary to the local bishop and after his death his picture was enshrined. I was happy to say Mass before it.

This image shed tears of blood on the Feast of

St Patrick, national patron of Ireland, 17 March, 1697, the worst year in the history of the Catholic Church in our country. For the 250th anniversary of the miracle, the great Cardinal Mindszenty spoke at Györ. When Pope John Paul II was in Hungary he prayed before the Irish Madonna. I hope that Mgr Tütto's book will stir thought and sentiments about Our Lady which we, Irish and his Hungarian fellow-countrymen, share.

Michael O'Carroll, CSSp.
Blackrock College, Dublin,
12 December, Feast of Our Lady of Guadalupe

Introduction

In choosing the title for my reflections on Our Lady's role as Teacher of Jesus I was inspired by her apparitions at Medjugorje where for eighteen years she presented herself through her messages as Mother, Teacher and Model. These titles of the Mother of the Church are proposed by the Second Vatican Council's teaching on Our Lady's role in the life of the Church (*Lumen Gentium*, Ch. 8) and by subsequent papal teachings. The Council taught: *The Son whom she brought forth is he whom God placed as the firstborn among many brethren* (Cf Rom 8:29), *namely the faithful, in whose birth and education she co-operates with a maternal love* (No. 63). *In the most holy Virgin the Church has already reached that perfection whereby she exists without spot or wrinkle* (Cf Eph 5:27). *Yet the followers of Christ strive to increase in holiness by conquering sin. And so they raise their eyes to Mary who shines forth to the whole community of the elect as model of virtues. Devotedly meditating on her and contemplating her in the light of the Word made man, the Church with reverence enters more intimately into the supreme mystery of the*

Incarnation and becomes ever increasingly like her Spouse (No. 65).

Pope Paul VI in his Apostolic Exhortation *Marialis Cultus* gives a clear interpretation to the above texts: *Mary is not only an example for the whole Church in the exercise of divine worship but is also, clearly, a teacher of the spiritual life for individual Christians. The faithful at a very early date began to look to Mary and to imitate her in making their lives an act of worship of God and making their worship a commitment of their lives* (No. 21).

Pope John Paul II in his Encyclical letter *Redemptoris Mater* treats this subject at length, especially in the third part, *Maternal Mediation,* under the heading *Mary in the life of the Church and of every Christian* (Nos. 42-47). In No. 47 the Holy Father gives a summary of Mary's role as Mother, Teacher and Model:

At the Council Paul VI solemnly proclaimed that Mary is the Mother of the Church, 'that is, Mother of the entire Christian people, both faithful and pastors' (21 November 1964). Later, in 1968, in the Profession of Faith known as the 'Credo of the People of God', he restated this truth in an even more forceful way in these words: 'We believe that the Most Holy Mother of God, the new Eve, the Mother of the Church, carries on in heaven her maternal role with regard to the members of Christ, co-operating in the birth and development

*of divine life in the souls of the redeemed'...
Mary is present in the Church as the Mother of
Christ, and at the same time as that Mother whom
Christ, in the mystery of the Redemption, gave to
humanity in the person of the Apostle John. Thus,
in her new motherhood in the Spirit, Mary
embraces each and every one in the Church, and
embraces each and every one through the Church.
In this sense Mary, Mother of the Church, is also
the Church's model. Indeed, as Paul VI hopes
and asks, the Church must draw 'from the Virgin
Mother of God the most authentic form of perfect
imitation of Christ'.*

The late Cardinal Hans Urs von Balthasar,
considered as one of the greatest theologians of
our time, has interpreted the teaching role of Our
Lady with reference to Our Lady's apparitions of
recent times in his booklet *Mary for Today*
(St Paul Publications, 1987), his contribution for
the Marian Year of 1987/88. He wrote a special
chapter with the title: *Mary, the Teacher of the
Church*, from which I am quoting the following
passage:

*It is only in heaven that we shall appreciate
how much the Church owes to Mary in understanding the faith, and indeed the 'simple' much
more than the 'clever and wise'. It would thus be
impossible to write a history of Mary's teaching
through the centuries. But we can venture to say
something about the sense and meaning of the*

17

apparitions of Our Lady that have been so many in recent times. Because Mary was so contemplative on earth, says Adrienne von Speyr, she can be so active in heaven, namely by letting the Church share in the superabundance of her memory...

Again and again in recent Marian apparitions the rosary has played a part: it has happened that Mary has fingered the beads along with those praying the rosary. Why should this be? So that we should prefer to pray to her and not to Christ or to the Father? On the contrary, so that it is from her point of view, from her memory that we should look at the mysteries of Jesus's life, and thereby at those of the trinitarian embodiment of salvation. Our eyes are bleary and dull: if you will forgive the metaphor, we must put on Mary's spectacles in order to see exactly (pp. 43-44).

The manifestation of Our Lady's threefold role as Mother, Teacher and Model through Medjugorje is a unique phenomenon in the history of the Church. The question arises: Why now, at the end of the Second Millennium? Many people are preoccupied with the thought of the Second Coming of Christ, implying the end of the world with all its cataclysm. I am inclined to a more positive interpretation of the Coming of Christ in a new way, through the members of his Body the Church, to restore mankind's faith in God, to renew the face of the earth by a new *Pentecost* and to establish the reign of Christ in all hearts. In the words of Pope John Paul II, this is the Advent period of the Church before the 2000th birthday of Jesus, the Saviour of the world, and Mary's presence in this period is of vital importance: *With good reason at the end of this Millennium, we Christians who know that the providential plan of the Most Holy Trinity is the central reality of Revelation and of faith feel the need to emphasize the **unique presence of the Mother of Christ** in history, especially during these last years leading up to the year 2000* (*Redemptoris Mater*, No. 3). The coming of Christ into our world in a new way, through the members of the Church, is at the heart of the message of Medjugorje where Mary, through her teaching mission, is helping us to become images of Christ, to become witnesses to Christ's presence in our world. Mary received this role at the foot of the Cross when Jesus entrusted his Church to her, in the person of the beloved disciple: '*Woman, behold your son...*' (Jn 19:26-27).

Why did Jesus entrust all of us to his Mother? Because he wanted us to be helped by her as he was helped by Mary during the thirty years of hidden life in preparing himself for his saving mission. That is the reason why this study is entitled *Mary, the Teacher of Jesus*. It is an essential part of the mystery of the Incarnation that the Son of God, the Word made man, was entrusted by God the Father, through the Holy Spirit, to a human being, to Mary of Nazareth, to be born of her, to be nursed and brought up by her. Jesus experienced the joys and blessings of having a wonderful Mother and only he knows how much he received from her. His gratitude to his Mother may be recognised in his final gesture before he died by giving us Mary to be our Mother too, to receive from her all the love and wisdom which he had received from her himself.

One may ask perhaps a more pertinent question: why did Jesus entrust all of us to his Mother just before he died on the Cross? Why did Jesus want his Mother to be present at the most terrifying form of execution, the crucifixion? No man – who is facing his execution – would wish his mother to witness the agony of his death. Yet, Jesus allowed his Mother to experience the agony of the birth of the new creation, to witness the opening of the Redeemer's side and heart from which the New Eve was born, Mary the model of the Church, the Mother of all living. Mary, who participated in the mystery of the Incarnation in a unique manner, was called as the first disciple of Jesus to be completely united with her Lord and Saviour in his 'hour' which became her 'hour' too. We all are called by virtue of our Baptism to participate in the saving work of our Redeemer, but the Blessed Virgin Mary, the Mother of our Redeemer, was called, in a unique manner, to share in the redeeming work of Jesus. Perhaps this may be the strongest reason for Mary's title 'Co-redemptrix', not in the sense of being equal to Jesus, the only Redeemer of the world, but being his 'associate' in the work of redemption. (Cf *Lumen Gentium* Nos. 58-63).

Being completely one with her Son in her work of redemption, Our Lady is also sharing in the teaching and evangelizing mission of Jesus in a special and unique way, through her maternal mediation, since Jesus Christ is the only one Teacher of salvation (Cf Mt 23:10).

In order to appreciate Our Lady's love for us as our Mother, Teacher and Model, it may be very helpful to us to reflect on Mary's relationship to her Son Jesus as his Teacher and Model. This idea is not new, of course. Pope John Paul II, in the Apostolic Exhortation *Catechesi Tradendae* about catechesis in our time (16 October 1979), in entrusting the catechising Church to Our Lady, writes the following: *By a unique vocation, she [Our Lady] saw her Son Jesus 'increase in wisdom and in stature and in favour'* (Lk 2:52). *As he sat on her lap and later as he listened to her throughout the hidden life of Nazareth, this Son, who was 'the only Son of the Father', 'full of grace and truth', was formed by her in human knowledge of the Scriptures and of the history of God's plan for his people, and in adoration of the Father* (Cf Jn 1:14; Heb 10:5). *She in turn was the first of his disciples.*

She was the first in time, because even when she found her adolescent Son in the Temple she received from him lessons that she kept in her heart (Lk 2:51). *She was the first disciple above all else because no one has been 'taught by God'* (Cf Jn 6:45) *to such depth. She was 'both mother and disciple', as St Augustine said of her, venturing to add that her discipleship was more important for her than her motherhood. There are good grounds for the statement made in the Synod Hall that Mary is a 'living catechism' and 'the Mother and Model of catechists'* (No. 73).

When Pope Paul VI visited Nazareth during his pilgrimage to the Holy Land in January 1964, he talked about the Holy Family's home as the school of the Gospel, implying Our Lady's teaching role: *The home of Nazareth is the school where we begin to understand the life of Jesus – the school of the Gospel... How gladly would I become a child again, and go to school once more in this humble and sublime school of Nazareth: close to Mary, I wish I could make a fresh start at learning the true science of life and the higher wisdom of divine truths* (*Divine Office*, Feast of the Holy Family).

There is another reason for reflecting on the relationship of Jesus and Mary during the hidden life at Nazareth, especially during the formative years of Jesus. In recent years Marian theologians have contributed towards a deeper understanding of Mary's role in the realm of salvation as *Co-redemptrix, Mediatrix* and *Advocate*, paving the way towards a possible papal definition. These studies are based on scriptural, patristic and theological resources, confirmed by papal documents and conciliar statements, which see Mary's relationship to Jesus in its entirety regarding her role in the Mystery of Salvation. For instance, *Lumen Gentium* (No. 61), describing Mary's role as *the generous associate and humble handmaid of the Lord states: She conceived, brought forth, and nourished Christ, she presented him to the Father in the Temple, shared her Son's sufferings as he died on the cross. Thus in a wholly singular way she co-operated by her obedience, faith, hope and burning charity.* The thirty years of hidden life is very much an essential part of the mystery of Salvation, even if the sources and documents remain silent on the hidden life of Jesus with the exception of the few episodes told by St Luke and St Matthew.

My special reason for this present study was prompted by the call of the Holy Father, Pope John Paul II to the whole Church to prepare for the Great Jubilee Year of 2000 by a three year programme of Trinitarian devotion, as proposed in his Apostolic letter *Tertio Millennio Adveniente*: (No. 40) *The first year, 1997, will be devoted to reflection on Christ, the Word of God, made man by the power of the Holy Spirit. The distinctly*

Christological character of the Jubilee needs to be emphasized, for it will celebrate the Incarnation and coming into the world of the Son of God, the mystery of salvation for all mankind. The general theme proposed by many Cardinals and Bishops for this year is: 'Jesus Christ, the one Saviour of the world, yesterday, today and forever (Cf Heb 13:8).

Our Lady's place in the first year's devotion is especially emphasized by the Holy Father (No. 43): *The Blessed Virgin who will be as it were 'indirectly' present in the whole preparatory phase, will be contemplated in this first year especially in the mystery of her Divine Motherhood. It was in her womb that the Word became flesh! The affirmation of the central place of Christ cannot therefore be separated from the recognition of the role played by his Most Holy Mother. Veneration of her, when properly understood, can in no way take away from 'the dignity and efficacy of Christ the one Mediator' (Lumen Gentium,* No. 62). *Mary in fact constantly points to her Divine Son and she is proposed to all believers as the model of faith which is put into practice. 'Devotedly meditating on her and contemplating her in the light of the Word made man, the Church with reverence enters more intimately into the supreme mystery of the Incarnation and becomes ever increasingly like her Spouse (Lumen Gentium,* No. 65).

In concluding the introduction to my reflections on Our Lady's role in her relationship to Jesus as his Teacher and Model, I wish to emphasize the importance of the phenomenon of Medjugorje. It seems to me that the Blessed Virgin Mary, the Queen of Peace as she calls herself, through her daily apparitions to the visionaries and through her messages, has established a school of prayer and love, a kind of 'Spiritual Nazareth' for our time. May the importance of Our Lady's mission through Medjugorje be recognised in the whole Church by the Jubilee Year 2000. Our Blessed Mother through her messages – which are in fact those of the Gospel expressed in the language of a mother – is helping us to be moulded into the likeness of Jesus, as she said in her message on 5 June 1986: *'Dear children, I especially desire that you all be the reflection of Jesus which will enlighten this unfaithful world walking in darkness. I want you to be a light for everyone and to bear witness to the Light...'*

Holy Scripture confirms that we are to be moulded into the likeness of Jesus: *'God decided beforehand who were the ones destined to be moulded to the pattern of his Son, so that he should be the eldest of many brothers'* (Rom 8:29).

It is my sincere belief that the Blessed Virgin Mary is revealing herself through Medjugorje as a unique 'teacher of the spiritual life' (Cf *Marialis Cultus*, No. 21) because she exercised the same role for Jesus before becoming the first of his disciples. My present study concentrates on her teaching role in the life of Jesus, especially during his adolescent years. Through her messages given at Medjugorje we may learn about the spirituality of Jesus of Nazareth, the Son of God and Son of Mary whom we are to emulate in becoming his reflection. The 'School of Nazareth' has a special significance for this moment of history as we are called to prepare, in the spirit of the 'hidden life' of Jesus, for the great Jubilee Year of 2000 and for the third Millennium of the Church of God.

I

'Who do you say I am?'

There is an important episode in St Matthew's Gospel when Jesus put this question to his disciples, 'Who do people say the Son of man is?' After receiving a variety of answers he asked his own disciples: *'Who do you say I am?' Simon Peter spoke up and said, 'You are the Christ, the Son of the living God'. Jesus replied, 'Simon, son of Jonah, you are a happy man! Because it was not flesh and blood that revealed this to you but my Father in heaven'* (Mt 16:13-20).

This episode indicates that Jesus as a man was fully aware of his divine identity, the Son of God who became Son of man, the Messiah, one with the Father, as many passages in St John's Gospel bear witness to this truth.

The big question is this: When and how did Jesus of Nazareth, in his human understanding, become aware and fully conscious of his divine identity? If the answer were that he was always aware of his divinity since the moment of Incarnation, then many problems could arise regarding the doctrine of the Incarnation. Holy Scripture in several instances insists that the incarnate Son of God became truly man as all human beings are, and not just in appearance.

St Paul in Philippians 2:5-8 says: *Make your own the mind of Christ Jesus: who, being in the form of God, did not count equality with God something to be grasped. But he emptied himself, taking the form of a slave, becoming as human beings are; and being in every way like a human being, he was humbler yet, even to accepting death on a cross.*

The Letter to the Hebrews (2:16-18) states the same truth about this self-emptying, 'kenosis': *It was not angels that he took to himself; he took to himself the line of Abraham. It was essential that he should in this way be made completely like his brothers so that he could become a compassionate and trustworthy high priest for their relationship to God, able to expiate the sins of the people. For the suffering he himself passed through while being put to the test enables him to help others when they are being put to the test.*

St Paul made a similar point in his letter to the Galatians (4:4-5): *When the completion of the time came, God sent his Son, born of a woman, born a subject of the Law, to redeem the subjects of the Law, so that we could receive adoption as sons.*

In his letter to Timothy, St Paul emphasized that Christ in his human nature is the only mediator between God and humanity: *There is only one*

God, and there is only one mediator between God and humanity, himself a human being, Christ Jesus, who offered himself as a ransom for all (1 Tim 2:5).

The great mystery of the Incarnation includes the down-to-earth reality of growing up, to develop, to learn, to become a mature human being, as St Luke mentions twice. First, after the presentation in the Temple: *The child grew to maturity being filled with wisdom, and the grace of God was upon him* (Lk 2:40). Then, after the episode of finding Jesus in the Temple, St Luke records that being subject to his parents, *Jesus progressed in wisdom and age and in grace before God and people* (Lk 2:52).

The episode of Jesus visiting his home town Nazareth shows in a special way that Jesus was known there as an ordinary working man and the people were scandalised when they saw him in a totally different light.

With the coming of the Sabbath he began teaching in the synagogue, and most of them were astonished when they heard him. They said, 'Where did the man get all this? What is this wisdom that he has been granted him, and these miracles that are worked through him? This is the carpenter, surely, the son of Mary, the brother of James and Joseph and Jude and Simon? His sisters, too, are they not here with us?' And they would not accept him. And Jesus said to them, 'A prophet is despised only in his own country, among his own relations and in his own house'; and he could work no miracle there, except that he cured a few sick people by laying his hands on them. He was amazed at their lack of faith (Mk 6:1-6).

Here we see that during his hidden life at Nazareth, in his contact with people, Jesus did not reveal in any way his divine nature. The question remains about his own awareness of his divine identity and about when he did become aware of it. The scene at the Jordan indicates that Jesus was conscious of his divine identity when he left home to be baptised by John the Baptist and from then on there is no question about the certainty that Jesus knew who he really was. But it is a legitimate question to ask, 'Since when, at what age did Jesus become aware of his divine identity?'

The relationship between the divine and human nature of Christ raised many questions from the earliest times, often leading to heresies condemned by the early Councils of the Church.

The first ecumenical Council of Nicea in 325 declared in its Creed that the Son of God is 'begotten, not made, of the same substance (*homoousios*) as the Father', and condemned Arius,[2] who had affirmed that the Son of God 'came to be from things that were not' and that he was 'from another substance' than that of the Father.

The Nestorian heresy[3] regarded Christ as a

human person joined to the divine person of God's Son. The third ecumenical Council of Ephesus in 431 defined 'that the Word, uniting to himself in his person the flesh animated by a rational soul, became man', from his conception. For this reason the Council of Ephesus proclaimed that Mary truly became the Mother of God (*Theotokos*) by the human conception of the Son of God in her womb.

The Monophysites[4] affirmed that the human nature had ceased to exist as such in Christ when the divine person of God's Son assumed it. Faced with this heresy, the fourth ecumenical Council of Chalcedon in 451 asserted: *Following the holy Fathers, we unanimously teach and confess one and the same Son, our Lord Jesus Christ: the same perfect in divinity and perfect in humanity, the same truly God and truly man, composed of rational soul and body; consubstantial with the Father as to his divinity and consubstantial with us as to his humanity; 'like us in all things but sin'. He was begotten from the Father before all ages as to his divinity and in these last days, for us and for our salvation, was born as to his humanity of the Virgin Mary, the Mother of God* (Cf *Catechism of the Catholic Church*, Nos. 465-469).

Besides these theological considerations, there are other aspects of the relationship between the divine and human nature in Christ which caused the Fathers of the early Church to reflect on this mystery.

St Athanasius (296-373), Bishop of Alexandria, in his Letter to Epictetus (5-9) emphasises Mary's part in the Mystery of the Incarnation:

The Word 'took to himself descent from Abraham', as the Apostle says, 'and therefore it was essential that he should in this way become completely like his brothers' (Heb 2:16), and take a body similar to us. That is why Mary is really part of his plan, so that he may take this body from her and offer it up for us as something that is his own. Accordingly, Scripture mentions his birth, and says: 'She wrapped him up in swaddling clothes'; the breasts that suckled him were called blessed; sacrifice was offered because he was the first-born. Gabriel announced the good news to Mary with all clarity: he did not say simply: 'what is born in you', in case it might be thought that the body had been introduced into her from outside; he said: 'what is born of you', so that it would be accepted that what she gave birth to, came from her in the natural way.

The Word took this course of action so that he could take on himself what was ours, offer it in sacrifice, and do away with it altogether, and then clothe us in what was his, as he inspired the Apostle to say: 'This perishable nature must put on the imperishable, and this mortal nature must put on immortality' (1 Cor 15:53).

This was no mere fiction, as some have thought. Far from it! Our Saviour really did become man, and this brought about the salvation of the whole man. Our salvation is no illusion, nor is it salvation of the body only: the salvation of the whole man, body and soul, was really brought about in the Word himself.

What was born of Mary, according to scripture, was by nature human; the Lord's body was a real one – real, because it was the same as ours. This was so because Mary was our sister, since we are all descended from Adam.

This is the meaning of John's words: 'The Word became flesh' (Jn 1:14), as can be seen from a similar passage in Paul: 'Christ became a curse for us' (Gal 3:13). The human body has been greatly enhanced through the fellowship and the union of the Word with it. From being mortal, it has become immortal; though physical, it has become spiritual; though made from the earth, it has passed through the gates of heaven.

Though the Word took a body from Mary, the Trinity remains a Trinity, and admits neither addition nor diminution. It is always perfect. In the Trinity one Godhead is acknowledged, and so in the Church one God is proclaimed, the Father of the Word (Divine Office, 1 January).

St Maximus the Confessor (580-662) in his work *Centuria* (Five Centuries) writing about the Mystery of the Incarnation poses the question, 'how can the same person be fully God by nature and become fully man by nature': *The great mystery of the divine incarnation always remains a mystery. In his essence the Word exists personally in the Father to the full: how is he in his person essentially in the flesh? How can the same person be fully God by nature and become fully man by nature, in no way deprived in either nature, neither in the divine nature by which he is God, nor in ours by which he became man? Only faith can grasp these mysteries, since it is the substance of things which are beyond intelligence and reason (Divine Office, 4 January).*

In my reflections on the humanity of Christ I am restricting myself to that period in the human life of Christ which can be described as the 'growing up period' (Cf Lk 2:40,52). Since the Word became fully man by nature, the humanity of Christ must have gone through the natural process of developing, growing up and maturing in his human potential of intellect, understanding, will, consciousness and emotions as does any other human being. My earlier question, however, must seek an answer: When and how did Jesus become aware, conscious – in his human understanding – of his divine identity and messianic mission for which he was preparing himself during the hidden life at Nazareth?

Jesus' awareness developed gradually, with the help of others, as every human being depends on the help of others for learning and developing potential. The main theme of this reflection is the role of the Blessed Virgin Mary, the Mother of Jesus, in helping him to come to understand his real identity and his mission. If the Second Divine Person, the Word, humbled himself to 'become flesh' in the womb of Mary and to suckle her breasts in order to live and grow, would it not be natural that Jesus depended on the wider maternal role of Mary in training and teaching him about matters which are essential to his self-understanding and to the understanding of his mission? Mary was the only human witness to the truth about Jesus's origin and his future mission (Cf Lk 1:26-38). In entrusting his Son to Mary, the Father in Heaven willed that Mary should be instrumental in helping Jesus in preparing for his mission. The great act of Incarnation was God's doing alone through the power of the Holy Spirit, but from then on God used a human channel, Mary, to give his Son to the world as its Saviour. I have already quoted the Apostolic Exhortation *Catechesi Tradendae* of Pope John Paul II about Mary's role in 'forming Jesus in human knowledge of the Scriptures and of the history of God's plan for his people, and in adoration of the Father' (No. 73), but, later on, I shall attempt to reflect more deeply on Mary's teaching role for Jesus. First, however, I would like to give a brief summary of the Church's teaching on some aspects of the hidden life of Jesus as presented in the *Catechism of the Catholic Church*.

II

'The hidden life of Jesus' in the *Catechism of the Catholic Church*

The Catechism treats the hidden life of Jesus in a general way. It makes reference to the homily of Pope Paul VI in Nazareth on 5 January 1964 about the home of Nazareth as the school of the Gospel in terms of 'lesson of silence', 'lesson on family life', 'lesson of work'. This implies Mary's special role without elaborating on it. Prior to that chapter, *The Catechism* gives some teaching on the relationship between the divine and human nature in Christ. I am quoting a few paragraphs on this subject (*in italics*), adding some comments.

Jesus

No. 430. *Jesus means in Hebrew: 'God saves.' At the annunciation, the angel Gabriel gave him the name Jesus as his proper name, which expresses both his identity and his mission. Since God alone can forgive sins, it is God who, in Jesus his eternal*

Son made man, 'will save his people from their sins' (Mt 1:21). *In Jesus, God recapitulates all of his history of salvation on behalf of men.*

Mary at the annunciation and visitation, Joseph in his vision have learnt about the divine identity of Jesus and about his messianic mission, although they could not comprehend this great mystery of the Incarnation. In their humility they could only consent to God's holy will, Mary with her 'fiat', and Joseph by 'taking Mary his wife to his home'. They were familiar with the prophecies of old about the human birth, growth and spiritual development of the Messiah as foretold by the prophet Isaiah, and about the names attributed to him which conveyed to them that the person born of Mary is a Divine Person:

The Lord will give you a sign. Behold, the virgin shall concieve and bear a son whom she will call Immanuel [God-with-us]. On curds and honey will he feed until he knows how to refuse the evil and choose the good (Is 7:14-15).

A son has been born for us, a son has been given to us, and dominion has been laid on his shoulders; 'Wonder-Counsellor, Mighty-God, Eternal-Father, Prince-of-Peace', to extend his dominion in boundless peace, over the throne of David and over his kingdom to make it secure and sustain it in fair judgement and integrity. From this time onwards and for ever, the jealous love of Yahweh Sabaoth will do this (Is 9:5-6).

How is the Son of God man?

In No. 470, in answer, *The Catechism* refers to the Vatican Council's document *Gaudium et Spes,* No. 22 §2: *Because 'human nature was assumed, not absorbed', in the mysterious union of the Incarnation, the Church was led over the course of centuries to confess the full reality of Christ's human soul, with its operations of intellect and will, and of his human body. In parallel fashion, she had to recall on each occasion that Christ's human nature belongs, as his own, to the divine person of the Son of God, who assumed it. Everything that Christ is and does in this nature derives from 'one of the Trinity'. The Son of God therefore communicates to his humanity his own personal mode of existence in the Trinity. In his soul as in his body, Christ thus expresses humanly the divine ways of the Trinity.'* The Catechism explains this by quoting the document: *'The Son of God... worked with human hands; he thought with a human mind. He acted with a human will, and with a human heart he loved. Born of the Virgin Mary, he has truly been made one of us, like to us in all things except sin'* (Cf Heb 4:15). The document, in the same paragraph, puts this mystery of the two natures into simple words: *He who is 'the image of the invisible God'* (Col 1:15), *is himself the perfect man. To the sons of Adam he restores the divine likeness which had been disfigured from the first sin onward.*

The Catechism continues in reflecting on Christ's soul and his human knowledge and will:

No. 471. *Apollinarius of Laodicaea asserted that in Christ the divine Word had replaced the soul or spirit. Against this error the Church confessed that the eternal Son also assumed a rational, human soul.*

No. 472. *This human soul that the Son of God assumed is endowed with a true human knowledge. As such, this knowledge could not in itself be unlimited: it was exercised in the historical conditions of his existence in space and time. This is why the Son of God could, when be became man, 'increase in wisdom and in stature, and in favour with God and man'* (Lk 2:52), *and would even have to inquire for himself about what one in the human condition can learn only from experience* (Cf Mk 6:38; 8:27; Jn 11:34; etc.). *This corresponded to the reality of his voluntary emptying of himself, taking 'the form of a slave'* (Phil 2:7).

The question I have to refer to again and again concerning the relationship between the divine and human nature in Christ is about Christ's awareness of the divine mysteries in his human knowledge. In Nos. 473 and 474, *The Catechism* states that *'the Son of God made man had the intimate and immediate knowledge of his Father'* (Cf Mk 14:36; Mt 11:27; Jn 1:18; 8:55; etc.); *'the Son in his human knowledge also showed the*

40

divine penetration he had into the secret thoughts of human hearts' (Cf Mk 2:8; Jn 2:25; 6:61; etc); and *'By its union to the divine wisdom in the person of the Word incarnate, Christ enjoyed in his human knowledge the fullness of understanding of the eternal plans he had come to reveal'* (Cf Mk 8:31; 9:31; 10:33-34; 14:18-20, 26-30).

The scripture passages with reference to the above statements are showing us Jesus in the fullness of his messianic mission, but they do not give answer to the question: if Jesus in his human knowledge and understanding was subject to the laws of human nature in order to 'increase in wisdom and in stature...', when did he come to 'the intimate and immediate knowledge of his Father and God's eternal plans'? In the next paragraph, *The Catechism* speaks of a progressive manifestation of Christ's divine nature, but it does not throw any light on the progressive, gradual nature of becoming aware – in Jesus' human self-understanding – of his divine identity.

No. 486. *The Father's only Son, conceived as man in the womb of the Virgin Mary, is 'Christ', that is to say, anointed by the Holy Spirit, from the beginning of his human existence, though the manifestation of this fact takes place only **progressively**: to the shepherds, to the magi, to John the Baptist, to the disciples. Thus the whole life of Jesus Christ will make manifest 'how God*

41

anointed Jesus of Nazareth with the Holy Spirit and with power' (Acts 10:38).

Regarding the human will in Christ, *The Catechism*, No. 475, states the following: *Similarly, at the sixth ecumenical council, Constantinople III in 681, the Church confessed that Christ possesses two wills and two natural operations, divine and human. They are not opposed to each other, but co-operate in such a way that the Word made flesh willed humanly in obedience to his Father all that he had decided divinely with the Father and the Holy Spirit for our salvation. Christ's human will 'does not resist or oppose but rather submits to his divine and almighty will'.*

The mysteries of Jesus' infancy and hidden life

In Nos. 522-534 *The Catechism* interprets the various episodes, as told us in the Gospels, in the light of the general salvation history. The hidden life of Jesus is summarised briefly, emphasising his obedience to his parents: *During the greater part of his life Jesus shared the condition of the vast majority of human beings: a daily life spent without evident greatness, a life of manual labour. His religious life was that of a Jew obedient to the law of God, a life in the community. From this whole period it is revealed to us that Jesus was 'obedient' to his parents and that he 'increased in wisdom and in stature, and in favour with God and man'* (Lk 2:51-52).

The important moment in the hidden life of Jesus comes when he is found in the Temple, and he speaks of his divine Sonship. No. 534. *The finding of Jesus in the temple is the only event that breaks the silence of the Gospels about the hidden years of Jesus. Here Jesus let us catch a glimpse of the mystery of his total consecration to a mission that flows from his divine Sonship: 'Did you not know that I must be about my Father's work?' Mary and Joseph did not understand these words, but they accepted them in faith. Mary 'kept all these things in her heart' during the years Jesus remained hidden in the silence of an ordinary life.*

The Catechism leaves many questions unanswered. Did the remark of Jesus in the Temple come as if totally out of the blue without any background to the story? Did Mary and Joseph live a life of pretence in the home of Nazareth, both knowing the truth about the divine Sonship of Jesus but never talking about it with him, especially at the time of his 'coming of age', before reaching the 'age of maturity' at twelve or thirteen when he became *Bar Mitzvah*, 'Son of the Covenant'? I just cannot think that the Holy Family lived 'in silence of an ordinary life' without sharing their heart's deepest sentiments with each other, especially when reflecting daily on Holy Scripture. The life of the Holy Family must have been the most beautiful school of prayer and love where Jesus, with the help of his Mother and foster-father, prepared himself for his messianic mission. The Gospels tell us nothing about this aspect of the life of Jesus, but then the Gospels do not contain everything about the life and work of Jesus, as St John stated at the end of his Gospel: *There was much else that Jesus did; if it were written down in detail, I do not suppose the world itself would hold all the books that would be written* (Jn 21:25).

I shall attempt in the following chapters to reflect on the 'School of Nazareth'. I am guided by the deep desire to get to know Jesus of Nazareth, the Son of God made man as much as possible, in the light of Mary's role in the life of Jesus, especially during these years of Trinitarian preparation for the great Jubilee of the Incarnation, year 2000. I hope and pray that the reader too may benefit from these reflections, so that with the help of our Blessed Mother Mary we may be able to do from the heart all that she is inspiring us to do, mindful of her original words: 'Do whatever my Son tells you' (Jn 2:5).

III

Jesus, 'Bar Mitzvah', the 'Son of the Covenant'

Growing to maturity

Between the presentation and finding of Jesus in the Temple there were twelve years which St Luke summarizes in these words: *As the child grew to maturity, he was filled with wisdom; and God's favour was with him* (Lk 2:40). The Book of Proverbs describes the way of obtaining true wisdom and God's favour: *And now, my children, listen to me. Happy are those who keep my ways. Listen to instruction and become wise, do not reject it. Blessed, whoever listens to me, who day after day keeps watch at my gates to guard my portals. For whoever finds me finds life, and obtains the favour of God* (Prov 8:32-35).

Jesus grew to maturity, increasing in knowledge and wisdom gradually, following the ways of human nature. Origen, an early father of the Church (+ 255), in his Homily on Jeremiah (I.7), applies to Christ the words of the prophet *'I do not know how to speak, for I am too young'* (Jer 1:6). *Jesus, before he became a grown man, while still a little child, since he 'abased himself'* (Cf Phil 2:8), *made progress; for no one makes progress if he is already perfect – progress implies the need of progress ...having 'abased himself', he then took back the things of which he had stripped himself, for he has done this as a voluntary act...*

According to Origen, therefore, Jesus, as human being, has gradually obtained wisdom and all 'the things' of which he, the Son of God, the Second Divine Person of the Holy Trinity, 'emptied himself' by becoming a human being. I have already indicated how Jesus revealed and manifested his divine nature and power during his messianic mission, but we are reflecting now on the formative years of Jesus as he 'grew to maturity'. 'Filled with wisdom' should not be understood that the child Jesus at the age of twelve has reached the state of 'perfect wisdom', because after the episode of finding him in the Temple, St Luke remarks again: *Jesus increased in wisdom, in stature, and in favour with God and with people* (Lk 2:52).

At what precise moment Jesus did become fully aware of his divine identity and of his messianic mission before he appeared in public, remains a mystery. The important truth for us to realise is that 'growing to maturity' was not a pretence by Jesus, but a fully human experience, and it is not against the teaching of the Church,

46

therefore, to raise questions about the humanity of Christ in its developing years, questions which perhaps were not raised in the past, mainly because the 'hidden life' of Jesus was not in the foreground of theological investigation. Since the role of the Blessed Virgin Mary in the realm of salvation came into prominence, especially since the Second Vatican Council, questions come to our minds which centre on the hidden life of Jesus. Here the role of Mary and Joseph was of paramount importance. When we consider that Jesus spent thirty years with his Mother and only three years in public, the purpose of the hidden life of Jesus in preparation for his messianic mission presents us with new inspiration. We are called to prepare for the Third Millennium of God's Church, renewing the saving mission of Jesus in a special way for our world which is dangerously moving away from God and from his laws.

Before we consider the environment in which Jesus 'grew to maturity', we keep in mind that in Jesus we see the 'perfect human being' (Cf *Gaudium at Spes,* No. 22, §2), free of original sin and of all its consequences, whose mind and soul were not handicapped like us, sinful, mortal creatures. Sin makes us less than human. Sin distorted the 'image of God' in us in which man was originally created (Cf Gen 1:27). Jesus is *the image of the unseen God, the first-born of all creation, for in him were created all things in heaven and on earth, everything visible and everything invisible* (Col 1:15). The flowing of God's grace and the working of the Holy Spirit found no resistance in the human heart and soul of the young Jesus. How all this may have affected his development, his humanity's mental and spiritual sensitivity and capacity is beyond our comprehension. On the other hand, we must be careful not to indulge in supposing super-human, miraculous or divine behaviour on the part of the child Jesus as we may find it in apocryphal gospels and in some other pious writings. The following basic truths about the Incarnation as stated in Holy Scripture should be kept in mind:

1. *The Word became flesh* (Jn 1:14). The Second Divine Person *became* a human being, with human mind and soul, and not just appearing in human form.

2. St Luke writes about the growth and spiritual development of the child Jesus: *As the child grew to maturity, he was filled with wisdom; and God's favour was with him* (Lk 2:40). *And Jesus increased in wisdom, in stature, and in favour with God and with people* (Lk 2:52).

3. St Paul's teaching on the mystery of the Incarnation:
    a. *When the completion of the time came, God*

*sent his Son, born of a woman, born a subject
of the Law, to redeem the subjects of the
Law, so that we could receive adoption as sons*
(Gal 4:4-5).

b. The Second Divine Person emptied himself
(*Kenosis*) of his divine glory, humbled himself
by becoming a human being: *Make your own
the mind of Christ Jesus: Who, being in the
form of God, did not count equality with God
something to be held onto. But he emptied
himself, taking the form of a slave, becoming
as human beings are; and being in every way
like a human being, he was humbler yet, even
to accepting death, death on a cross* (Phil 2:5-
8). The 'self-emptying' of the Second Divine
Person by becoming 'as human beings are'
does not refer to the times of Jesus' sufferings
only, but to his whole human life, from the
moment of conception.

c. Christ as 'human being' is the only mediator
between God and humanity: *There is only one
mediator between God and humanity, himself
a human being, Christ Jesus, who offered
himself as a ransom for all* (1 Tim.2:5).

4. By sharing our human nature, Jesus became
like us in everything, except sin.

a. *Since all the children share the same human
nature, Christ too shared equally in it, so that
by his death he could set aside him who held*

the power of death, namely the devil, and set free all those who had been held in slavery all their lives by the fear of death. For it was not the angels that he took to himself; he took to himself the line of Abraham. It was essential that he should in this way be made completely like his brothers so that he could become a compassionate and trustworthy high priest for their relationship to God, able to expiate the sins of the people (Heb 2:14-17).

b. *The high priest we have is not incapable of feeling our weaknesses with us, but has been put to the test in exactly the same way as ourselves, apart from sin* (Heb 4:15).

Finally, we must keep in mind that the Mother of Jesus, the Immaculate Virgin Mary, was also free of original sin and of all its consequences. Her relationship to Jesus, therefore, was a unique mother-child relationship which may have had a much deeper intensity in many areas of that relationship than we can imagine. She looked after Jesus as any other good mother does, but she saw in her child also her Lord and Saviour. This must have affected her attitude and behaviour very deeply indeed. The child Jesus must have been greatly influenced in his growth and development by such a loving Mother and we shall reflect on this in the subsequent chapters.

The 'School of Nazareth'

The home of Nazareth was the ideal place for the child Jesus to grow up, to be filled with wisdom and to walk in God's favour. We know that the young Jesus did not attend any special school because the townsfolk would have known about it and they were surprised and even driven to evil plans against Jesus when they heard him speaking in the synagogue (Cf Mt 13:53-58; Mk 6:1-6). Yet, Jesus had the best of schools and the best of teachers in the home of Mary and Joseph. Their special responsibility was the education of Jesus and to prepare him especially for his 'coming of age' at the age of twelve or thirteen when, as an adult, he was obliged to follow all the commands of the Mosaic Law and was also called upon to take part in the synagogue services.

Joseph, as the head of the family, would have ensured that Jesus learned about everything that the Mosaic Law prescribed, besides teaching him his own trade of carpentry. During his public life when Jesus visited Nazareth he was referred to as the 'carpenter, the son of Mary' (Mk 6:3). Joseph may have died some years before and Jesus as a carpenter was the bread-winner until he left home to start his messianic mission.

The Saviour of the world having sanctified manual labour by his own share in it, the Church wanted to emphasize the holiness of human work when Pope Pius XII made the first day of May a solemn Feast of St Joseph the Worker. At the beginning of the Second Vatican Council there was a significant event with reference to St Joseph. The Bishop of Mostar, Petar Cule, in whose diocese Medjugorje is situated, on 10 November 1962, put in a long plea for the inclusion of the name of St Joseph in the Canon of the Mass (now the First Eucharistic Prayer). Many of the Council Fathers expressed their irritation and he was stopped by the presiding Cardinal. Fortunately, Pope John XXIII was listening to the debates on closed circuit television in his apartments. Perhaps it was the brusque cutting-off of Bishop Cule that may have prompted the Pope to issue a motu proprio decree three days later, on 13 November effective from 8 December 1962, ordering the insertion of the name of St Joseph in the Canon of the Mass. The Bishop's heartfelt wish was granted.

Regarding Joseph's role in teaching the young Jesus all that the Law prescribed, we should keep in mind the strict rule given by God through Moses to his people: *Listen, Israel: Yahweh our God is the one, the only Yahweh. You must love Yahweh your God with all your heart, with all your soul, with all your strength. Let the words I enjoin on you today stay in your heart. You shall tell them to your children, and keep on telling them, when you are sitting at home, when you are out and about, when you are lying down and when you are standing up; you must fasten them on your hand as a sign and on your forehead as a headband; you must write them on the doorposts of your house and on your gates* (Deut 6:4-9). Joseph, 'being a just man' (Cf Mt.1:19), was faithful indeed to God's laws, and we can imagine that in the home of Nazareth everything was motivated by fulfilling God's holy will.

The most important influence for the spiritual formation of a child in Israel was the home within a highly active religious community, which was guided by 613 biblically ordained commandments, most of which regulated the Sabbath rest and the many seasonal feasts and celebrations. These religious festivities expressed the essential life and history of God's chosen people. The ways and means of celebrating the festivities were totally Scripture-based, and as such they were most suited to teach a child to understand and live his or her faith.

Jesus in the house of his Father (Lk 2:40-52)

When a male Israelite attained his religious majority, he was obliged to observe all the commandments which are contained in the *Torah*, the first five books of the Old Testament. In addition, he was obliged to make pilgrimage to

Jerusalem three times a year, for the Feast of Passover, Pentecost and Tabernacles, as ordained by God: *Three times a year all your menfolk must appear before Yahweh your God in the place chosen by him: at the feast of Unleavened Bread* (Passover), *at the Feast of Weeks* (Pentecost), *at the feast of Shelters* (Tabernacles). *No one must appear empty-handed before Yahweh, but each must give what he can, in proportion to the blessing which Yahweh your God has bestowed on you* (Deut 16:16).

The transition from boyhood to manhood has been traditionally observed by being called up to read from Torah in the synagogue, and by wearing the phylacteries when he recites his daily morning prayers. The phylacteries are leather cubes which contain small parchment strips on which are inscribed verses and some commands from the Scripture (Cf Deut 6:8).

According to the prevailing view of Jewish scholars there is no evidence that at the time of Jesus the 'coming of age' event was celebrated in any special way. According to them the celebration of becoming *Bar Mitzvah*, 'Son of the Covenant', on reaching adulthood at the age of thirteen, is of a much later origin among the Jews. On the other hand, when we consider how strictly the Israelites held on to their traditions and how strictly God's laws were kept regarding the three annual pilgrimages to Jerusalem by the menfolk, it is unthinkable to assume that reaching religious maturity at a certain age was no special event in the life of a male Israelite. I use the term 'Israelite' instead of 'Jew' (Cf Jn 1:47), because at the time of Jesus the word 'Jew' was applied only to the tribe of Juda, the people living in Judaea, the Judaeans, the Jews as we find it in St John's Gospel. Later, all the followers of the Law of Moses were called Jews.

When St Luke tells us about Jesus at the age of twelve making his pilgrimage to Jerusalem for the feast of the Passover (not the first time I assume), perhaps he wanted to make the point that Jesus reached adulthood that entitled him to join the group of pupils and listeners at the discussion of scribes and teachers in the Temple. Did he celebrate the occasion of his 'coming of age' with his parents during the earlier part of the festivities? It is possible. This gave Jesus the opportunity to put his newly acquired rights into practice when he stayed behind in Jerusalem instead of returning home. The effect must have been extraordinary as St Luke tells us: *They (Mary and Joseph) found him in the Temple, sitting among the teachers, listening to them, and asking them questions; and all those who heard him were astounded at his intelligence and his replies* (Lk 2:46-47).

One may wonder what the discussions were about. Most of the scribes and teachers were still remembering all the excitement, some years back, caused by the visit of the Magi searching for the 'infant king of the Jews' (Cf Mt 2:1-12). When King Herod asked the chief priests and scribes about where the Christ (Messiah) was to be born, they told him, 'at Bethlehem in Judaea'. One may assume that the question about the Messiah must have been still a burning issue among the scholars at the time of the young Jesus' visit to the Temple. The teachers of the Law were grouped around two rabbinical schools, opposing each other. The more liberal and gentler school of interpretation was led by Hillel and his grandson, Gamaliel (Cf Acts 5:34-40; 22:3). The other school was led by Shammai who interpreted the Mosaic Law very strictly and rigidly. As Shammai and his disciples were very intolerant towards the Gentiles, they were in frequent conflict with the Roman authorities.

Assuming that the discussion in the Temple court may have been on the question whether the 'infant king of the Jews' as the Messiah was still alive, one might think that the Shammaites would dismiss his existence on the ground that King Herod, 'realising that he had been fooled by the wise men', had all the male children of Bethlehem and its surrounding district killed who were two years old or less (Cf Mt 2:16-18). Jesus may have argued that God had often saved his chosen ones from disaster like Noah, Lot and their families, and others, so one could believe that the Messiah had come and in due time he would appear before the people. Whatever Jesus may have said, Scripture states that *all those who heard him were astounded at his intelligence and his replies* (Lk 2:47).

How did Jesus come to make such an impact? Was his human intelligence at work, or did he reveal his divine knowledge? One might think of the latter when we consider his answer to Mary's question: *'My child, why have you done this to us? See how worried your father and I have been, looking for you.' He replied, 'Why were you looking for me? Did you not know that I must be busy with my Father's affairs?' But they did not understand what he meant* (Lk 2:48-50). This last sentence may refer to the teachers as well, not just to the parents of Jesus. It appears that this is the first manifestation of his consciousness of being the 'Son of God'. The big question is, when did Jesus become conscious of being the Son of God? Was his divine self-knowledge at work in the Temple and did he become aware, in his human understanding, of being the Son of God during his years of development in the home of Nazareth? We must try to find an answer to this question even though some theological opinions on this subject raise more problems rather than give a satisfactory answer to my question.

Views of theologians on Christ's human intelligence

The biblical scholar, Marie Joseph Lagrange OP (1855-1938), in *The Gospel of Jesus Christ*,[5] commenting on the above episode in St Luke's Gospel, writes:

'As for his human intelligence, we learn from sound teaching of theology, which alone can guide us here, that from the first moment of his conception there had been granted to Jesus the highest degree of that *clear vision of God* which is promised to the saints in heaven. But his human nature, though united to the divine person, nevertheless exercises freely all the actions proper to itself; nor did this gift of the *beatific vision* hinder his human intellect from exercising that faculty of acquiring knowledge which is customary in those growing up to manhood. St Luke is careful to state this explicitly, for without it the whole gospel would be unintelligible and would be no more than a continual make-believe.

He has also given us to understand that at the age of twelve Jesus was fully conscious of his divine origin. The evangelists in no way attribute this consciousness to revelation or to a process of gradual growth. It must be therefore attributed to that *direct vision of God* which Jesus enjoyed from the very beginning of his life, for by that alone could his human intelligence have been enabled to fathom the distinction between Father, Son and Holy Ghost in the bosom of the ineffable Trinity.'

It is very difficult to reconcile the above text with the scriptural criteria under which we should consider the Church's teaching on the Incarnation, as mentioned before. One may understand the theologian's effort to try to avoid the idea of limiting the 'perfection' of the Son of God. The issue here, however, is not about how the divine nature in Christ was operating even during his infancy, but about how can we understand the 'self-emptying' (kenosis) of the Second Divine Person in becoming 'like us in everything except sin' (Cf Heb 4:15), and how may we interpret the two important passages in St Luke's Gospel referring to Jesus 'growing to maturity' and 'increase in wisdom, in stature, and in favour with God and with people' (2:40, 52).

In his Apostolic Exhortation *Catechesi Tradendae* Pope John Paul II wrote about Our Lady's role in teaching Jesus: *By a unique vocation, she saw her Son Jesus 'increase in wisdom and in stature, and in favour'. As he sat on her lap and later as he listened to her throughout the hidden life of Nazareth, this Son, who was 'the only Son of the Father', 'full of grace and truth', was formed by her in human knowledge of the Scriptures and of the history of God's plan for his people, and in adoration of the Father* (No. 73).

If we accept Lagrange's interpretation, one might think of an embarrassing situation when the young Jesus would say: *Mother, don't bother, I know it all. Don't you know that I am God and that I know everything*? Or, if he would say nothing, just pretending to learn from Mary, is this the way we should understand the 'human intelligence' of Jesus, switching to 'divine intelligence' whenever it would suit him? I just cannot think that there was any pretence in the Holy Family. Of course, I accept, as I stated before, that the answer of Jesus to his parents in the Temple revealed that he was conscious of his divine origin. As to the question of how he came to this consciousness in his human understanding, there might be an answer other than Lagrange's view about Jesus' 'direct vision of God' which I shall try to explain in the next chapters.

The biblical scholar, Dr Franz Michel Willam, in *Mary the Mother of Jesus*,[6] under the heading *Mary the Spiritual Guide of the Boy Jesus*, writes the following:

'Jesus, who was truly the Son of God, assumed human nature, and was therefore truly man, like us in all things except sin (Cf Heb 4:15). As a human being, Jesus experienced a spiritual development; he grew from childhood to boyhood and from boyhood to manhood; like other men he gathered new experiences of life. This experimental knowledge existed in him side by side with the *infused knowledge* which he possessed from the beginning. Hence we may rightly speak in general of his human development, and in particular of the religious development of his human nature, keeping in mind at all times that the veil of mystery will never be entirely removed from the life of his soul...

'How mysterious was the life of Jesus and Mary during those years when the Child was awaking to its own spiritual life! Jesus was the Child who, more than any other of the children of men, lived in the *most intimate union with God*; his divinity was united to his humanity, filling all the phases of his human life.'

Again, we are confronted with the same problem of reconciling the teaching of Holy Scripture on the Incarnation with Dr Willam's view of Jesus having 'infused knowledge', 'most intimate union with God', from the beginning of his human existence. How could he 'grow and increase in wisdom' if he – in his human consciousness – had the divine knowledge all the time?

The answer to this question may be found in the teaching of the eminent theologian Karl Rahner, SJ (1904-1985). In his *Encyclopedia of Theology*,[7] he states two important qualifications which make all the difference in our understanding of the nature of Christ's human knowledge, keeping always in mind that all this still remains a great mystery.

First, this 'direct vision of God' must not be identified with the beatific vision of the Risen Christ.

Secondly, while this 'direct vision of God' is a fundamental reality in the human soul of Christ, resulting from the personal (hypostatic) union of his human soul with the Second Person of the Holy Trinity, its manifestation in perception and language is subject to the natural process of development of the human nature of Christ (Cf Lk 2:40; 52).

For the sake of fidelity to Rahner's characteristic way of describing metaphysical concepts, I quote the relevant text from the Encyclopedia with slight adaptation of some philosophical terms.[8]

§5. Jesus Christ's knowledge and freedom in his humanity.

'Although it is not a defined dogma, the Church teaches that from the beginning of its existence the human soul of Jesus had a direct vision of God. To understand this, we need to remember the fundamental and essential condition of Jesus as a real human being.

'Being' and 'consciousness' are mutually related, and so an immediate relation to God in the form of this direct vision inevitably follows from the fact that his human nature was essentially (hypostatically) united with God. We can leave aside the fact that this direct vision of God does not need to be simply identified with the beatific vision, which the Risen Christ enjoyed.

But even then this fundamental and, in a certain sense, transcendental condition (namely, that Christ's existence entailed a most radical and unique relationship with God) does not mean that it must always have been explicitly reflected upon in all its implications and made the object of conscious thought. That would be simply incompatible with an honest exegesis of Luke 2:52; Mark 13:32; Matthew 16:28.

But it also means that this fundamental condition, which is the only basis on which Jesus can speak, can only be explicitly reflected upon and made the object of conscious thought or put into words in the context of his historical experience, with the terms and concepts of the time and place in which he lived, and so with the human openness of his history. On this basis it is not impossible to assume a development in this 'translation' of his fundamental condition into a more explicit consciousness and so into words. We may still be able to see traces of this development in the Synoptics.

When we consider the Eucharistic Mystery through which Our Lord gave himself to us in the form of bread to nourish us for the eternal life, we can sense the infinite humility and vulnerability of God in coming into our world to 'dwell among us' (Cf Jn 1:14), revealing what the infinite Love of God is capable of doing for our sake. Through the mystery of the Incarnation, God became man, he became human in every way, excepting sin. Reflecting that sin makes us less than human, we must look at Jesus in his humanity as the 'perfect man' without sin. It was in the mind of God from all eternity in creating human beings in the image of himself. We are contemplating the sinless Mother's sinless Son who is also the Second Person of the Holy Trinity. This divine Person, however, in his humility chose to reveal himself in Jesus of Nazareth gradually, in a human way, following the natural laws of growth and development, understanding, knowledge and self-awareness, 'growing to maturity, increasing in wisdom, in stature, and in favour with God and with people'. This is the path I am trying to trace in my present reflections.

IV

Adoration of the Father

As he sat on her lap and later as he listened to her throughout the hidden life of Nazareth, this Son, who was 'the only Son of the Father', 'full of grace and truth', was formed by her in human knowledge of the Scriptures and of the history of God's plan for his people, and in adoration of the Father (Catechesi Tradendae, No. 73).

The Holy Family at prayer

The basic religious activity of an Israelite family was the obligatory prayer at least in the morning and in the evening. The prayer of an Israelite was not just a prayer to God but prayer to Yahweh, the God of Israel, the God of Abraham, Isaac and Jacob to whom he or she could speak with childlike confidence and intimacy, expressing personal feelings freely in a very human way, even complaining sometimes against God. The Old Testament writings are full of the most expressive and moving prayers, manifestations of the human heart. The prayers of Moses, of the

Prophets, of holy men and women, above all, the hundred and fifty psalms, are the most telling evidence that prayer for an Israelite was the most important expression of a living faith in Yahweh, and of his or her relationship to him.

In the Hebrew language there are many different words used to describe the various sentiments, elements and modes of prayer, such as prayers of petition, asking for favours, mercy or forgiveness; prayers of praise, thanksgiving, blessing and exaltation; prayers of meditation, contemplation and adoration. The psalms contain the greatest variety of prayers for every occasion, used privately or publicly, prayers which people knew by heart.

Keeping in mind the extraordinary experiences of Mary and Joseph in receiving revelation concerning the divine origin of Jesus and his mission in God's plan, we realize how important a part prayer played in the home of Nazareth. Mary and Joseph deeply believed that the best formation of the child Jesus would be achieved through an intense prayer life as channel of divine assistance. Praying together as a family in the morning and evening, and at other times as well, reciting or singing the psalms which Jesus learned by heart, must have been a very intimate experience for Jesus to feel the love which surrounded him, and the grace flowing into his heart from Yahweh whom he soon would call 'Abba, Father'.

As a child, Jesus may have noticed that his parents often spent a long time in silent prayer and he must have noticed the peace and joy radiating from their quiet encounter with God. I am sure Jesus was drawn by this kind of prayer from his earliest days and later on, during his public life, he often spent whole nights in silent contemplation, in union with his heavenly Father.

The Holy Family may have talked about the importance of such prayer and Jesus may have asked his Mother to teach him this kind of prayer which she calls 'prayer of the heart' or 'praying with the heart' in her many messages given at Medjugorje. Prayer of the heart is the unceasing prayer which enables us to be in a continual prayerful state of mind and heart. Through Medjugorje, Mary teaches us her way of praying. This is my main reason for asserting that she taught Jesus to pray with the heart, the unceasing prayer. St Luke says about Our Lady, the Contemplative, twice: *As for Mary, she treasured all these things and pondered them in her heart* (Lk 2:19; 51).

I quote just one of many of Our Lady's messages at Medjugorje on prayer of the heart:

Dear Children, today I am calling you to prayer. I am always calling you, but you are still far away. Therefore, from today, decide seriously to dedicate time to God. I am with you and I wish to teach you to pray with the heart. In prayer of the heart you will encounter God. Therefore, dear children, pray, pray, pray! Thank you for responding to my call (25 October 1989).

Our Lady often used the expression 'pray, pray, pray' and once she explained its meaning: *When I say 'pray, pray, pray', I do not mean only increase the hours of prayer, but increase the desire to pray and to be in contact with God, to be in a continuously prayerful state of mind* (26 June 1984).

Saying prayers, learnt by heart, such as the psalms, can easily lead to mechanical recitation of prayers without interior attention. Jesus may have noticed very early in his life how some people made a show of saying their prayer. This made him later explain to his disciples the prayer which pleases God: *When you pray, do not imitate the hypocrites: they love to say their prayers standing up in the synagogues and at the street corners for people to see them. In truth I tell you, they have had their reward. But when you pray, go to your private room, shut yourself in, and so pray to your Father who is in that secret place, and your Father who sees all that is done in secret will reward you* (Mt 6:5-6).

Jesus had strong words against the pharisees, too, about their way of praying, by priding themselves on being upright and despising everyone else, as in the parable of the pharisee and the tax collector (Lk 18:9-14), or, by wearing broader headbands (phylacteries) and longer tassels on their cloaks, not just during the time of prayer but always, to impress people with their devotion (Cf Mt 23:1-7).

Seeing Jesus praying in a quiet place, after he had finished, his disciples asked him to teach them to pray (Cf Lk 11:1). They knew their prayers, they prayed like any devout Israelite several times during the day, but they wanted to learn the way Jesus prayed. So, Jesus taught them how to pray (Cf Mt 6:9-13; Lk 11:1-4). He told them that prayer, coming from the heart, should be an expression of deep father-child relationship which does not need many words. The *Our Father* is a short prayer, but one could dwell on each word for a long time, to make it into a prayer of the heart indeed.

In conclusion, we can safely say that prayer became for Jesus a dialogue with the heavenly Father, taught and inspired by his Mother. How deep this dialogue would lead him, we shall reflect on later. It is sufficient for us to realise that prayer, prayer of the heart, the unceasing prayer, must have been the most important feature in the spiritual development of the young Jesus.

The Sabbath[9]

Besides intensive prayer life within the Holy Family, religious celebrations were the most suitable opportunities for the young Jesus to understand the history of his people and God's plan of salvation for all mankind. Since the religious celebrations in the life of the Israelites were guided by God's ordinances contained in the Sacred Scriptures, they were the best means in the hands of Mary and Joseph to 'form Jesus in human knowledge of the Scriptures and of the history of God's plan for his people, and in adoration of the Father'. Everything Jesus did and said during his public mission was rooted in the Old Testament. The events, the celebrations and prophecies were all pointing to their fulfilment in the life and work of Jesus, the Messiah. Mary and Joseph knew about those prophetic words and signs referring to their Son, Jesus. The expectation of the Messiah in the public conscience provided the ground for them to draw the attention of Jesus to the scripture passages about God's Anointed One, the Christ, the Messiah whom he will send to save his people and all mankind.

There were many feasts throughout the year, the major ones lasting for a week. Most of them were celebrated in remembrance of important events in the history of God's people. The most common celebration affecting the life of the family was, however, the celebration of the Sabbath, the seventh day of the week, the day of rest, both in the home and in the local synagogue, the house of prayer. The local community gathered there for public worship and for instruction in Sacred Scripture, especially in the Torah, the Law, the first five books of the Bible, containing all God's commandments and ordinances. The Scriptures were interpreted in the language of the local congregation.

Although the religion of the Israelites focused on the sanctuary in the Temple of Jerusalem, the force of circumstances, first in the Exile, and later among the scattered Jewish communities throughout the world, the local synagogue became for all practical purposes the centre of worship. Because of the laws governing the Sabbath rest, especially in view of the limited distance one was allowed to walk on the Sabbath, every small community had its own synagogue. In Jerusalem, for instance, at the time of Christ, there were over four hundred synagogues.

'Keeping the Sabbath holy' was so fundamental a concept in the life of the Israelites that it took precedence over the entire system of the Law, sometimes even over the law of charity which caused Jesus on many occasions to challenge the legalistic mentality of his contemporaries by healing the sick on the Sabbath. This is how God's ordinance about the Sabbath, the third in the Ten Commandments, was known and observed accordingly:

Observe the Sabbath day and keep it holy, as

Yahweh your God has commanded you. Labour for six days, doing all your work, but the seventh day is a Sabbath for Yahweh your God. You must not do any work that day, neither you, nor your son, nor your daughter, nor your servants – male or female – nor your ox, nor your donkey, nor any of your animals, nor the foreigner who has made his home with you; so that your servants, male and female, may rest, as you do. Remember that you were once a slave in Egypt, and that Yahweh your God brought you out of there with mighty hand and outstretched arm; this is why Yahweh your God has commanded you to keep the Sabbath day (Deut 5:12-15).

In its original purpose, for an Israelite, the Sabbath meant a liberation from the mundane and a consecration of the sacred, linking the Israelites in an eternal bond of faith with God the Creator. His symbolic cessation of divine activity after six days is commemorated every seventh day as a supreme act of faith in the Creator. Through the study of Sacred Scripture, meditation and discourse on the Law of God, the Sabbath offered an opportunity for moral regeneration and ongoing renewal of faith. In the home of Nazareth the observance of the Sabbath must have been a deeply spiritual experience for Jesus who, later in his public life wanted to help people to appreciate the real meaning of the Sabbath, that it is lawful to do good for others on the Sabbath

(Cf Mt 12:12) and that 'the Sabbath was made for man, not man for the Sabbath' (Cf Mk 2:27).

The celebration of the Sabbath began on Friday evening. In later periods the celebration of the Sabbath became a very elaborate ceremonial, full of symbolism, especially by the use of various candles like the seven-branched *Menorah*, the symbol of Judaism, and the *Havdala* candle marking the end of the Sabbath. Even in the time of Jesus, however, the home was the scene of meaningful rituals. The housewife had the honour of ushering in the holy day by kindling the Sabbath lights before sunset on Friday afternoon. Just as the darkness, described at the beginning of Genesis, was swept away by the words 'Let there be light' when God divided the light from the darkness (Gen 1:3-5), so did Mary symbolically separate this day from the other six days of the week by lighting the Sabbath lamp at the beginning of Sabbath, while Jesus stood at her side. Her husband, Joseph, would light the special *Havdala* candle to mark the end of the Sabbath.

These ceremonies were accompanied by prayers thanking God for the gift of the day of rest and for the life-giving light God gave during the six days of creation. The Sabbath lamp also represents *shalom bayit*, the peace of the home, following an ancient saying 'where there is light, there is peace'. The glow of the Sabbath lights in the home on Sabbath eve served to remind each

73

member of the family that the sacred day had arrived and must be observed with reverence, care and love.

The ceremony of lights would have made a deep impression on Jesus who, later on in his public life, called himself the 'Light of the world' (Jn 8:12) and called also his followers to be light for the world (Cf Mt 5:14).

Our Lady in her messages at Medjugorje has often reminded us that we are to be a light for others who are walking in darkness. This is what being a 'reflection of Jesus' means as she told us on 5 June 1986 (*see* Introduction).

Besides the Sabbath lights, bread and wine were also indispensable elements at the Sabbath eve meal, at the luncheon feast the following day, and also at other festive rituals. The first Sabbath eve meal ritual was the *Kiddush* which means 'sanctification' and designates the formal ritual performed by the head of the household over a cup of wine upon his return from the Sabbath eve synagogue service. In this way the Sabbath was formally proclaimed and the home life of the Israelite family is consecrated. For the Kiddush the master of the house usually stands, holding the Kiddush beaker in his right hand. The Kiddush benediction itself emphasizes both the religious and the national significance of the Sabbath. It includes texts from the Bible describing God's day of rest, underlining the belief that the universe is the product of God's work, not chance, and it includes references to Israel's redemption from Egypt and to God as the Redeemer. The father of the house is then seated and he and all those at the table drink from the cup.

After Kiddush came the ritual washing of the hands. The ceremony, a symbolic purification, preceded the partaking of bread at every meal and is related to the ceremonial washing of hands in the Temple prior to the priestly service. The home of an Israelite family was regarded as a 'little sanctuary', and was compared to the Temple, and the dining table was likened to a sacrificial altar.

The Sabbath bread, baked by the woman of the house, was also special: the two braided *Hallah loaves* were set out to provide the first morsels for the meal at Sabbath eve and Sabbath day. They commemorated the double portions of manna gathered by the Israelites in the wilderness for the Sabbath, on their way to the Promised Land (Cf Exodus 16:5).

The significance of using bread and wine in these celebrations goes back to the time of Abraham. Following the victory over the rulers of the land the Lord God promised him, Melchizedek, the king and high priest of Salem (Jerusalem) offered bread and wine and pronounced his blessing: *Blessed be Abraham by God Most High, Creator of heaven and earth. And blessed be God*

BhaiDod;

Most High for putting your enemies into your clutches (Gen 14:19).

One may assume that at the Sabbath eve celebration Psalm 104(103), the hymn to God the Creator, may have been recited or sung to thank God for all his gifts of food, symbolized by bread and wine.

Sabbath and the Eucharist

When we consider how much the celebration of the Sabbath in the Holy Family must have meant for Jesus, we can understand that he, the High Priest of the New Covenant 'according to the order of Melchizedek' (Cf Heb 5:6,10; 6:20; 7:17, 20-28) established the sacrificial meal of the New Testament by uniting the Sabbath eve meal with the celebration of the Paschal Lamb as a memorial of his own sacrifice on the cross as the Lamb of God.

Following the miracle of the loaves, Jesus explained how he, the bread of life will be the new manna on our life's journey towards our eternal home of Heaven (Cf Jn 6). The day of his Resurrection became our Sabbath, in remembrance of the *new creation in Christ* (Cf 2 Cor 5:17), and the Eucharist became our Sabbath eve meal for giving thanks and praise to God for our redemption from the slavery of sin, and for all God's gifts. His Body is our *Hallah loaf*, his Blood is our *Kiddush* (Cf 1 Cor 10:16-17), and Jesus is our *Shalom bayit*, our peace and reconciliation (Cf Eph 2:14-16).

We should also consider the Marian dimension of the Eucharist. The first miracle of Jesus was performed through the intervention and intercession of Mary at the wedding of Cana when Jesus changed water into wine in abundance (Jn 2:1-11). This first miracle was the inaugural sign of the Eucharist. At the last banquet of his life, at the Last Supper, Jesus changed wine into his blood, in the 'blessing cup' of the New Covenant (Cf 1 Cor 10:16). The words of Jesus spoken at Cana, 'My hour has not yet come', have a special significance for Mary. The whole Eucharistic Mystery in John's Gospel, including the sacrifice of Christ on the cross, is referred to as the 'hour of Jesus' (Jn 13:1) which became also the 'hour of Mary' when she became the New Eve, the 'Mother of all living', as the dying Lord Jesus entrusted to her his Church in the person of John (Jn 19:26-27).

Since the Body and Blood of Jesus are of the body and blood of Mary, 'born of the virgin Mary' as we profess in the Creed, and, since the glorious Body of Jesus in Heaven is the same Body which Mary gave him: born in Bethlehem, died on Calvary, placed in the sepulchre and risen from there but assuming the glorified form, and being offered in sacrifice on our altars, Mary is also the 'Mother of the Eucharist' as she calls herself in a message through Father Stefano Gobbi.[10] In the same message she calls herself also the Mother of the Incarnation, the Mother of the Redemption and the Mother of Jesus the Priest.

Mary invites us through her messages at Medjugorje to participate in the Eucharist in a special way by living the Holy Mass:

Dear Children, I wish to call upon you to live the Holy Mass. There are many among you who have experienced the beauty of the Mass, but there are also others who come rather reluctantly. I have chosen you, dear children, but Jesus is the one who gives his graces in the Mass. Therefore, live consciously the Holy Mass and let your coming to it be a joyful one. Come and accept Holy Mass with joyful love (3 April 1986).

Holy years and festivals

Besides the weekly Sabbath celebrations a very important formative influence on the young Jesus were the national festivals, calling to mind the historical events in the life of God's chosen people. Perhaps the most unusual and longest festivals were the Holy Years, the *Sabbatical Year* every seventh year, and the *Year of Jubilee*, every fiftieth year, the year of liberation, the year of many favours and graces, as described in the Book of Leviticus, chapter 25. Whether Jesus experienced the celebration of a Jubilee Year, we don't know, but he must have been familiar with its meaning since at the beginning of his public life he proclaimed his mission as a 'year of favour from the Lord': *The Spirit of the Lord is on me, for he has anointed me to bring the good news to the afflicted. He has sent me to proclaim liberty to captives, sight to the blind, to let the oppressed go free, to proclaim a year of favour from the Lord* (Lk 4:18-19).

Going through the calendar year which for the Israelites began in the month of *Nisan* or Abib (March-April), I mention only the major festivals, celebrated according to God's ordinances (Cf Lev 23, Deut 16).

On 14 *Nisan* the *Feast of Passover* was celebrated when the roasted paschal lamb was eaten in the evening and the *Week of Unleavened Bread* began in remembrance of Israel's redemption from Egyptian bondage and of the triumphant exodus into the wilderness. The highlight of the Paschal celebration was the *Seder*, a joyous and ritual meal during which was the reading of the *Hagadah* by the parents to their children, the story of the Exodus and the accompanying miracles. The *Seder* meal included bitter herbs as well in remembrance of the hardships during their wandering through the wilderness. The celebration was divided into four parts, marked by four cups of wine, accompanied by singing of psalms. For Jesus, the celebration of the Passover feast was the most important annual festival from the moment in his youth when he became aware of his messianic mission. Especially from the writings of the prophet Isaiah (ch. 53). He knew that the fulfilment of the Passover mystery, the real redemption of all mankind would be achieved by himself when he would be the Paschal Lamb sacrificed on the cross.

Fifty days later, from the day after the Sabbath, *Pentecost* or the *Feast of Weeks* was celebrated, marking the close of the harvest; hence the Israelites were required to make offerings to Yahweh from the first-fruits, including two loaves made from the new cereal. By the time of Christ the feast also commemorated the event when God gave his people through Moses, on Mount Sinai, the Law they should live by. Jesus sent the Holy Spirit on his followers on *Pentecost* day, initiating the New Law, written not on stone tablets, but in the hearts of his disciples by the Holy Spirit, as foretold by the prophet Ezekiel: *I shall give you a new heart, and put a new spirit in you; I shall remove the heart of stone from your bodies and give you a heart of flesh instead. I shall put my spirit in you, and make you keep my laws, and respect and practise my judgements...You will be my people and I shall be your God* (Ez 36:26-28).

The Day of Atonement (*Kippurim*) was celebrated with fast and great solemnity on the 10th of the 7th month, *Tishri* (September-October). The ritual acts were performed by the high priest, of which the most important was his entering into the Holy of Holies, which took place only on this day. The writer of the letter to the Hebrews sees in the sacrifice of Christ the fulfilment of everything the Day of Atonement signified: *But now Christ has come, as the high priest of all the blessings which were to come. He has passed through the greater, the more perfect tent, not made by human hands, that is, not of this created order; and he has enetered the sanctuary once and for all, taking with him not the blood of goats and bull calves, but his own blood, having won an eternal redemption...* (Heb 9:11-14).

The Feast of Tabernacles or *Shelters*, lasting one week, was celebrated a few days later, from 15th to 22nd of *Tishri*. The object of the feast was to commemorate the forty years spent in the wilderness. Booths or shelters were erected in which people lived during the feast. The first and last days of the feast were days of public worship, and the intervening days were devoted to the free enjoyment of the festal season. Throughout the week an elaborate scheme of sacrificial offerings was carried through (Cf Lev 23:39-43). Part of the last day's celebration was the carrying of water from the pool of Siloam, outside Jerusalem, in solemn procession to the altar of sacrifices and the priests poured the water over the altar and on the temple ground while prayers were recited asking for God's blessing for the next fruitful year. In the temple ground a bare rock was visible which, according to a rabbinic tradition (Cf Num 20:8) followed the Israelites in the desert, providing water for their needs. For St Paul this rock symbolizes the pre-existent Christ already active in Israel's history (Cf 1 Cor 10:4). While water was poured over this rock in the temple ground, it was customary to read the account of the miracle of the water from the rock (Cf Ex 17:1-7).

For Jesus this ceremony had a very important meaning and on one occasion, on the last day of the celebrations, he spoke loudly about the living water which would be poured out from the hearts of those who believe in him. St John interpreted his words as referring to the Holy Spirit: *On the last day, the great day of the festival, Jesus stood and cried out: 'Let anyone who is thirsty come to me! Let anyone who believes in me come and drink! As Scripture says. "from his heart shall flow streams of living water".' He was speaking of the Spirit which those who believed in him were to receive; for there was no Spirit as yet because Jesus had not yet been glorified* (Jn: 37-39).

This caused great dispute among the Jews

(Judaeans) because some believed that Jesus is the Messiah, others would not believe because he is a Galilean, and the Messiah should be born in Bethlehem, in Judaea. Of course, they did not realize that Jesus was born in Bethlehem (Cf Jn 7:40-53).

There were other festivities like *Dedication of the Temple* in the month of *Kislev* (November–December), Feast of Esther and Feast of Purim in the month of *Adar* (February–March), commemorating the deliverance of the Israelites from Haman, who plotted their extermination throughout the Persian Empire. All these feastdays and celebrations helped the young Jesus to learn about the history of his people, and later, during his public life, to give them deeper meaning by seeing those events foreshadowing their fulfilment in himself. For us, by seeing the Holy Scripture of the Old Testament in this light, we are helped to appreciate and understand the New Testament even more. That is why Our Lady at Medjugorje often called us to read and pray Holy Scripture, and to keep the Bible in a special place in the home:

Dear Children, today I ask you to read the Bible in your homes every day. Keep it in a special place, where it will always remind you to read it and to pray. Thank you for having responded to my call (18 October 1984).

The school of the natural world

One of the striking features of Our Lord's way of teaching during his public ministry is the frequent usage of images and parables taken from the world of nature and from the countryside. His trade was carpentry, working among rural people. His preaching reveals his close familiarity with the ways of nature. When he spoke about divine providence, he used the analogy of flowers in the fields (Mt 6:28-31). When speaking about the kingdom of God, Jesus used images from the countryside, from the life of farmers and fishermen, like the sower, darnel among the wheat, the mustard seed, the birds of the air, the dragnet (Cf Mt 13).

How did Jesus come to such appreciation of the world of nature around him? One obvious answer would be his familiarity with Holy Scripture, especially the psalms and various hymns which are full of God's praise through the works of his creation. One of the most beautiful hymns of such praise is the song of the three young men (Dan 3:56-88) which Jesus must have prayed many times from his earliest days in adoring his heavenly Father through the works of his creation.

Jesus may have also read the passage from the book of Sirach which emphasises the importance of parables and proverbs in the life of a wise person:

The wise man concentrates his mind and his meditation on the Law of the Most High. He researches into the wisdom of the men of old, he occupies his time with the prophecies. He preserves the discourses of famous men, he is at home with the niceties of parables. He researches into the hidden sense of proverbs, he ponders the obscurities of parables (Sir 39:1-3).

Mary, the Mother of Jesus, must have played an important part in drawing the attention of the young Jesus to the beauty of nature where one can see the hand of God. She may have inspired Jesus to see God's goodness and wisdom through his creation and to praise God for his many gifts through nature. When he was small, he must have often been at the side of Mary when she worked in their garden to grow vegetables for the table, or flowers for the festivities. Our Lady's love for nature and her guidance for Jesus to appreciate the natural world may be recognised in some of her messages given at Medjugorje. The analogy of flowers can help us to change and come closer to God:

Dear Children, today I want to ask you to open your hearts to God, just like flowers in the spring yearning for the sun. I am your Mother and I would like you to be ever closer to the Father, and that he will always bestow abundant gifts on your hearts (31 January, 1985).

Dear Children, Today I call you to open

yourselves to God through prayer as a flower opens itself to the rays of the morning sun. My dear children, do not be afraid. I am with you and I intercede before God for each of you so that your heart may receive the gift of conversion. Only in this way, my dear children, will you understand the importance of grace in these times and God will become closer to you. Thank you for having responded to my call (25 April, 1998).

When the Gulf War started in January 1991, Our Lady warned against the grave danger threatening nature and our planet, referring to the use of poison gas and chemicals which are a constant threat to the world of nature we live in:

Dear Children, today as never before I am calling you to pray. Let your prayer be a prayer for peace. Satan is powerful and wants to destroy not only human life but also nature and the planet on which you live... (25 January, 1991).

V

The moment of truth

Looking back

Looking back on my reflections made so far, in summarizing, I touched on the various aspects of the mystery of the Incarnation, from various sources including Scripture, tradition and the teaching of the Church. I tried to highlight those important human conditions and circumstances, like the religious practices of the Israelites, in which the Child Jesus developed to maturity, growing in human understanding, knowledge and conduct of life, all of which is an essential part of the mystery of the Incarnation.

I touched on the theological problem of whether the divine nature of Christ may have played any role in the development of his human nature, since it is the teaching of the Church that 'by its union to the divine wisdom in the person of the Word incarnate, Christ enjoyed in his human knowledge the fullness of understanding of the eternal plans he had come to reveal' (*Catechism*, No. 474). I have emphasized the importance of the 'self-emptying' way of God's Son coming into our world (Cf Phil 2:7) to avoid any appearance or pretence of being fully human by secretly adhering to his divine nature. The idea of 'beatific vision' in Jesus of Nazareth, from the first moment of the Incarnation, advocated by some theologians is very difficult to reconcile with the Pauline thesis of 'self-emptying'. If Jesus Christ, in his human consciousness, had the 'beatific vision' from the first moment of his earthly existence, what form of vision should we attribute to him after the resurrection? Karl Rahner makes a distinction between the fundamental reality of divine knowledge in Jesus Christ and its manifestation in human understanding and language which is subject to the natural conditions of growing up and development. It seems to me that this is the answer to the theological problem mentioned above.

There is no doubt about Jesus' awareness of his divine identity during his public mission as many Scripture texts testify. My main question is, when did Jesus become aware, in his human understanding, of being the Son of God, the Second Divine Person? This is not a question about the fact and truth of Jesus Christ being the Second Divine Person from the moment of his human conception, but is a question about the nature of human understanding in Christ. This understanding was subject to the human human development and growth. Only in this way can we understand St Luke's words *growing to maturity and increasing in wisdom* (Lk 2:40, 52).

Jesus, therefore, must have come to an awareness of his divine identity *initially* in a human way, that is, with the help of Mary and Joseph who were entrusted by God the Father to bring him up and to help him to prepare for his messianic mission. I emphasize the word 'initially', because to become fully aware, in his human understanding, of his divine identity was possible for Jesus only by a special revelation from his Father through the workings of the Holy Spirit to whom the young Jesus of Nazareth opened himself completely, through deep prayer, prayer of the heart, as he learnt it from his Mother. More of this later.

As the young Jesus was approaching the 'coming of age' when he would be obliged to fulfil all the observances of the Law, Mary and Joseph may have felt that it was time that they shared with Jesus all they knew about his origin and real identity. Assuming that a very intimate and deeply spiritual relationship existed in the Holy Family, one would expect that Mary and Joseph, while reflecting on the many Scripture passages during their daily and weekly devotion and prayer, would have discussed their meaning with Jesus, especially the passages which refer to the life and work of the Messiah. My attempt to reflect on this intimate exchange in the Holy

Family is based on the simple desire to try to understand the humanity of Jesus in his developing years. In this way one may become even more aware of God's infinite goodness manifesting itself in the humble condition of a simple and poor working family preparing the Saviour of the world for his redeeming mission. Life in the Holy Family of Nazareth was a real human life of an ordinary working family which is not alien to our own experience. It is not necessary to have documented evidence for every phase of the life of Jesus on earth. We can visualise it as it might have happened. The truth of becoming aware of his divine identity is what matters, not the imagined details, as I try to answer the question of how Jesus, in his human understanding, may have become aware of his divine origin and mission.

Sharing the secret

At the age of eleven or twelve, Jesus must have been an extremely intelligent boy, judging by his performance in the Temple. Prior to that episode, I assume that Jesus must have asked many questions of Mary and Joseph about the Messiah whom everybody was awaiting. I can well imagine the scene when Mary and Joseph talked with each other about the need to tell Jesus the truth about himself and decided to tell him the facts, gently but truthfully. He would understand, he is old enough – they thought. They may have decided that Joseph would speak with Jesus first, and then Mary would do the rest. They must have prayed much about this decision.

Joseph and Jesus

I expect that the young Jesus learned his foster-father's trade, carpentry, because later on, after Joseph's death, he was the bread-winner and was known in Nazareth as the carpenter (Mk 6:3). Jesus must have spent much time with Joseph in the workshop and, besides work, they would have talked about many things. At an appropriate time in the life of the young Jesus, Joseph may have shared with Jesus his own experience, how the angel of the Lord appeared to him in a dream saying: *Joseph, son of David, do not be afraid to take Mary home as your wife, because she has conceived what is in her by the Holy Spirit. She will give birth to a son and you must name him Jesus, because he is the one who is to save his people from their sins* (Mt 1:18-25).

How Matthew learnt about Joseph's secret, whether from Mary or Jesus himself, we do not know, but we can safely assume that Mary and Joseph told it first to Jesus before anybody else. And it must have happened before they went up to Jerusalem for the feast of the Passover when Jesus was twelve years old and when he was already aware of his true identity and divine origin (Cf Lk 2:49).

How the young Jesus may have reacted to this revelation, we may only guess, comparing the situation perhaps with a foster-child in our time when he or she finds out who were the real parents. In the case of Jesus, he must have felt a tremendous joy, because through the behaviour of his parents towards him he must have sensed, in his human understanding, that he was someone special, and when he heard Joseph's story, it all became clear to him and he wanted to know more. So, Joseph may have told him the rest of the story about his birth in Bethlehem, the visit of the shepherds and Magi and about their flight to Egypt because King Herod wanted to kill him (Mt 2:1-15). Jesus may have been a few years old when they returned from Egypt, and so he may have remembered the return journey and the early years of his life in Nazareth. I do not wish to go into all the possible details of the story, because the important point in my reflection as to how Jesus became aware of his identity is the fact that *initially* it happened in a human way, through the testimony of Joseph and then of Mary. In fact, Joseph may have suggested to Jesus that he must ask his Mother, because she was his real earthly Mother who was chosen by God in a wonderful way.

Mary and Jesus

I imagine Mary was praying ardently to God while Joseph was speaking with their Son. Jesus, after leaving the workshop, may have run to his Mother with some excitement, from which Mary understood that Jesus learnt the truth about himself. Jesus, in his thirst for the whole truth, must have asked his Mother to tell him everything that she knew about his origin. Jesus sensed what a wonderful Mother he had and he was eager to hear from Mary's lips about God's marvellous work.

We can safely assume that whatever Mary told Luke about the origin and infancy of Jesus, she shared her secret first with her Son. So she may have told Jesus all that we know from St Luke's Gospel about the annunciation (Lk 1:26-38), her visitation to Elizabeth and the birth of John the Baptist (Lk 1:5-25, 39-80), the birth of Jesus at Bethlehem, the visit of the shepherds (Lk 2:1-21), and much more that is not in the Gospels.

The words of Mary would have left a deep impression in Jesus as she told him about how the heavenly messenger announced the joyful news to Mary:

Hail, O favoured one, the Lord is with you! Mary, do not be afraid; you have won God's favour. And behold, you will conceive in your womb and bear a son, and you shall call his name Jesus. He will be great, and will be called the Son of the Most High. The Lord God will give him the throne of his ancestor David; he will reign over the House of Jacob forever and of his kingdom there will be no end (Lk 1:28-33).

Mary may have told Jesus about how disturbed she was by these words, but the angel explained to her how her Son will be conceived:

The Holy Spirit will come upon you, and the power of the Most High will cover you with its shadow. And so the child will be holy and will be called Son of God (Lk 1:35).

Mary and the boy Jesus may have reflected on the prophecy, foretold by the prophet Isaiah, about the birth of the Messiah, and about how this prophecy has been fulfilled at the time of the annunciation:

The virgin is with child and will give birth to a son whom she will call Immanuel, God-with-us (Is 7:14).

Mary may have told Jesus also about the problem she faced: how to tell this to Joseph or anybody. Nobody would believe her. But she had great trust in God, gave her consent, and she knew that her life was now totally in God's hands. Joseph had already told Jesus how he learnt about Mary's secret, and Mary told Jesus how Elizabeth knew about her secret which dispelled all her worries when she heard Elizabeth's greeting at the time of her visit to Elizabeth and Zechariah:

Of all women you are the most blessed, and

blessed is the fruit of your womb. Why should I be honoured with a visit from the mother of my Lord? For behold, when the sound of your greeting came to my ears, the babe in my womb leaped for joy. And blessed is she who believed that the promise made her by the Lord would be fulfilled (Lk 1:42-45).

Mary would have told Jesus also about how Zechariah, after the power of speech returned to him, praised God and prophesied about the future of John on the occasion of his circumcision:

And you, little child, you shall be called Prophet of the Most High, for you will go before the Lord, to prepare a way for him, to give his people knowledge of salvation through the forgiveness of their sins, because of the faithful love of our God in which the rising Sun has come from on high to visit us, to give light to those who live in darkness and in the shadow of death, to guide our feet into the way of peace (Lk 1:76-79).

Again, Mary and Jesus may have reflected together on the prophecy about the mission of John and wondered when that prophecy will be fulfilled:

A voice of one that cries in the desert, 'Prepare a way for the Lord. Make a straight highway for our God across the wastelands. Let every valley be filled in, every mountain and hill be levelled, every cliff become a plateau, every escarpment a plain; then the glory of the Lord will be revealed and all humanity will see it together, for the mouth of the Lord has spoken' (Is 40:3-5).

I would assume that after such revelations and sharing, the Holy Family praised God with all their heart at their evening prayer. Mary and Joseph may have shown great joy knowing that Jesus is now aware of his true identity, and they may have reflected with joyful heart on the words of the Prophet Isaiah about the Son of God who became the Son of Mary and Joseph:

A son has been born for us, a son has been given to us, and dominion has been laid on his shoulders; and this is the name he has been given, 'Wonder-Counsellor, Mighty-God, Eternal-Father, Prince-of-Peace', to extend his dominion in boundless peace, over the throne of David and over his kingdom to make it secure and sustain it in fair judgement and integrity. From this time onwards and forever, the jealous love of the Lord of hosts will do this (Is. 9:5-6).

The Holy Family may have talked late into the night about the prophetic utterances concerning the Messiah and Jesus may have asked many questions before retiring to his alcove, not to sleep, but to pray to his heavenly Father.

Jesus, the Son of the Eternal Father

After receiving the marvellous revelations about his identity, Jesus, lifting up his arms towards heaven, would have expressed his gratitude to God, his Father in Heaven, for giving him such loving parents who were chosen to be instrumental in God's plan for the salvation of mankind. From the depth of his heart Jesus prayed to his Father to give him the light of the Holy Spirit in order to comprehend with his human understanding this great mystery of being the Son of God while being also the Son of Mary. Would it be wrong to assume that this may have been the moment that while Jesus being at deep prayer, experienced an ecstasy during which the heavenly Father revealed himself to his Son, enabling Jesus to become fully aware, in his human understanding, of his real identity as the Second Person of the Holy Trinity? This is what I meant when earlier I referred to Mary's and Joseph's part as the *initial* event for Jesus to discover his true identity. To become fully aware, in his human understanding and perception, of being the Son of God is possible only by the Father's revelation through the working of the Holy Spirit to whom the young Jesus opened himself in deep prayer, as he learnt it from his human parents.

During his public ministry, the heavenly Father confirmed the identity of his Son several times publicly. One should assume that God the Father revealed himself first to his own incarnate Son who is to fulfil the mission of redemption as the Redeemer of the world.

At the beginning of his messianic mission, after his Baptism in the river Jordan, the Father in heaven gave testimony about the identity of Jesus to John the Baptist who saw the Holy Spirit coming down on Jesus like a dove and heard the voice from heaven: *This is my Son, the Beloved; my favour rests on him* (Cf Mt 3:16-17; Jn 1:32-34). Later, on Mount Tabor, when Jesus was transfigured, the Father in heaven gave testimony about his Son to the principal apostles, Peter, John and James: *This is my Son, the Beloved; he enjoys my favour. Listen to him* (Cf Mt 17:1-8; Mk 9:2-8; Lk 9:28-36; 2 Pet 1:16-18). Shortly before Jesus suffered, he prayed aloud in the midst of the crowd, Father, glorify your name!, and the people heard the voice from heaven: *I have glorified it, and I will again glorify it* (Cf Jn 12:27-30).

So, in this light, we can understand that the young Jesus himself needed an affirmation from his heavenly Father to become fully aware of his divine identity, and this may have happened during the night after he had learned the truth from his parents about himself. I am not attempting to describe what Jesus may have experienced in such an encounter of supernatural nature. St Paul makes reference to his own supernatural experiences in Paradise and about divine revelations he received, but he does not want to boast about them (Cf 2 Cor 12:1-6). In his letter to the Galatians, however, he explains that the Gospel he is preaching did not come to him from any human testimony but through a revelation of Jesus Christ (Gal 1:11-20).

I mention the above instances to indicate that we cannot exclude the likelihood of divine revelation in the life of the young Jesus even if Holy Scripture is silent about it. At what depth such an experience may have enlightened his human understanding is beyond our comprehension. We must also keep in mind the Pauline thesis about the self-emptying of divine glory in the Son of God made man (Cf Phil 2:7). Whatever divine assistance the young Jesus may have received, it gave him such a self-confidence which may explain what happened in the Temple where his self-revelation started, surprising even his parents when he said to them: Did you not know that I must be in my Father's house? (Cf Lk 2:49).

After sharing their secret with their Son, Mary and Joseph may have noticed that Jesus was radiant and was talking with excitement about the forthcoming pilgrimage to the Temple of Jerusalem, as the Feast of the Passover was very close. In the mind of Jesus, the earthly 'dwelling-place' of his heavenly Father in the Temple may have received a very important significance for his future mission and he must have been very keen to go there to honour his heavenly Father in a special way. Jesus may have quoted the words of the Psalm, *I rejoiced that they said to me, 'Let us go to the house of the Lord'. At last our feet are standing at your gates, Jerusalem* (Ps 122). He may have thought of the words of another Psalm, *I am eaten up with zeal for your house* (Ps 69:9) which had a very dramatic manifestation later when in the beginning of his public life his first step in the Temple was to cleanse it from defilement. This provoked the anger of the Jews (Judaeans) which in turn gave Jesus the opportunity to prophesy about the Temple that was his body: *Destroy this Temple, and in three days I will raise it up...He was speaking of the Temple that was his body, and when Jesus rose from the dead, his disciples remembered that he had said this, and they believed the Scripture and what he had said* (Cf Jn 2:13-22; Mt 26:61).

The young Jesus, aware of his true identity, gave the first sign of his messianic mission in the Temple, but, after returning to Nazareth, he may have assured his parents that life must go on as before by simply being their child who had to grow to maturity and adulthood. St Luke summarized that life in these words: *He went down with them and came to Nazareth and lived under their authority. His mother stored up all these things in her heart. And Jesus increased in wisdom, in stature, and in favour with God and with people* (Lk 2:51-52).

* * * * *

The presence of Yahweh among his people, symbolized by the sanctuary in the Temple, the Holy of Holies, had a very important implication for the mission of Jesus through its fulfilment by his own presence among his people, and later by the Eucharistic presence in our churches. His last words to his followers, before ascending to heaven, were: *I am with you always; yes, to the end of time* (Mt 28:20).

In one of her messages at Medjugorje, Our Lady urged us to have great respect for the dwelling-place of the Lord, the church, where she wants to gather us and to lead us to God:

Dear Children, God wants to make you holy. Therefore, through me he is calling you for complete surrender. Let the Holy Mass be your life. Understand that the church is God's palace, the place where I gather you and want to show you the way to God. Come and pray! Do not look to others or speak ill of them, but rather let your life be a testimony on the road to holiness. Churches deserve respect and are set apart as holy because God, who became Man, dwells in them day and night. Therefore, dear children, believe and pray that the Father will strengthen your faith, and then ask for whatever you need. I am with you and I rejoice because of your conversion, and I am protecting you with my motherly mantle. Thank you for your response to my call (25 April, 1988).

VI

Mary, the first disciple of Jesus

"She in turn was the first of his disciples. She was the first in time, because even when she found her adolescent Son in the Temple she received from him lessons that she kept in her heart (Lk 2:51). *She was the first disciple above all else because no one has been 'taught by God'* (Cf Jn 6:45) *to such depth. She was 'both Mother and disciple', as St Augustine said of her, venturing to add that her discipleship was more important for her than her motherhood. There are good grounds for the statement made in the Synod Hall that Mary is a 'living catechism' and 'the Mother and Model of catechists'"* (*Catechesi Tradendae*, No. 73).

Return to Nazareth

Between the finding of Jesus in the Temple and his public appearance for Baptism by John the Baptist at the River Jordan there are eighteen years about which the Gospels are totally silent. St Luke sums up this whole period in a few words: *'He went down with them and came to Nazareth and lived under their authority. His mother stored up all these things in her heart. And Jesus increased in wisdom, in stature, and in favour with God and man'* (Lk 2:51-52).

The Catechism summarizes this greater part of the earthly life of Jesus in the following words: *'During the greater part of his life Jesus shared the condition of the vast majority of human beings: a daily life spent without evident greatness, a life of manual labour. His religious life was that of a Jew obedient to the law of God, a life in the community. From this whole period it is revealed to us that Jesus was 'obedient' to his parents and that he 'increased in wisdom and in stature, and in favour with God and man'* (No. 531).

This silent, hidden life, however, must have been a most important period for Jesus for preparing himself for his messianic mission. Prior to the episode in the Temple, Jesus – in his human understanding – became aware of his divine origin and identity. This was the subject of the previous chapter. During the second part of his hidden life, I believe, he became more and more aware of how his messianic mission was to be fulfilled, in accordance with the will of his heavenly Father.

At some point during this period his foster-father, Joseph, died, and Jesus became the bread-winner. He was known as 'the carpenter, the Son of Mary' (Cf Mk 6:3), when he visited Nazareth in the beginning of his public life. We can assume that Jesus and Mary spent quite a few years sharing many prayerful exchanges and reflections on Holy Scripture about the mission of the Messiah and Mary became more and more the disciple rather than the teacher of Jesus. In my effort to describe this period, I am using my own imagination again, although I try to adhere to the spirit of Holy Scripture. This is not intended to be a theological but rather a prayerful and devotional exercise as we try to visualise the hidden life of the Holy Family in Nazareth.

Mary's discipleship began in the Temple when Jesus said to his parents, *'Why were you looking for me? Did you not know that I must be in my Father's house?'* (Lk 2:49). After all the worries and desperate searching for him, the words of Jesus may have come to Mary and Joseph as a shock. Their journey back to Nazareth may have been a very quiet one, making Mary and Joseph realize that Jesus is no more a child. He had reached the age of maturity, to be treated accordingly, and perhaps Jesus wanted to make the point.

Even if his parents remained silent about the episode in the Temple, after settling down to the usual routine in their home in Nazareth, I expect Mary and Joseph were looking for an opportunity to tell Jesus the reason for their worries and anxieties when looking for him after the Passover. When an opportunity came, they may have told him about the episode when Jesus was presented in the Temple shortly after his birth, as the Law required. They recalled what the old Simeon prophesied about Jesus, holding him in his arms:

At last, all-powerful Master, you give leave to your servant to go in peace, according to your promise. For my eyes have seen your salvation which you have prepared for all nations, the light to enlighten the Gentiles and give glory to Israel, your people (Lk 2:29-32).

Then turning to Mary, Simeon continued: *Look, he is destined for the fall and for the rise of many in Israel, destined to be a sign that is opposed – and a sword will pierce your soul too – so that the secret thoughts of many may be laid bare* (Lk 2:33-35).

Mary and Joseph may have told Jesus how worried they were about him ever since that prophecy. They recalled the story of how King Herod wanted to kill him, how his soldiers killed all the little children of Bethlehem and its surrounding district, and why they had to flee to Egypt after the angel warned Joseph in a dream (Mt 2:13-18). When they were looking for him after the feast of the Passover, they may have told Jesus, they were filled with fear for him. And when they found him in the Temple among the teachers and scribes with their opposing views, they were even more terrified because there was a party of people called the Herodians, supporters of the Herod dynasty (Cf Mk 3:6), who might wish to kill anyone who claimed to be the Messiah. Fortunately, Mary and Joseph may have thought, the Herodians did not understand the words of Jesus when he said that he must be 'in his Father's house' (Lk 2:49).

Jesus must have been very upset by hearing about the murder of so many little children because of him and he must have thought much about the meaning of Simeon's prophecy about the rejection of the Messiah. If Jesus needed for his human development human assistance in order to learn about himself, we can assume that he needed again the initial help from Mary and Joseph in his human understanding about his future mission as the Messiah.

Again, I assume, in the light of Simeon's prophecy, Jesus may have turned in deep and heart-felt prayer to his heavenly Father, asking him to give him the enlightenment of the Holy Spirit about the meaning of this prophecy and about the meaning of various Scripture passages referring to the rejection and the suffering of the Messiah. In such a deep prayer Jesus would receive the divine wisdom to discern and fully understand the words of Holy Scripture about himself as the years went by, preparing himself for doing the Father's will.

The will of the Father

Jesus must have spent many prayerful hours in reflecting on what his heavenly Father's will was for him to fulfil his messianic mission. Gradually, as the years went by, in the light of Holy Scripture, through the inspiration of the Holy Spirit and through many conversations with his mother and foster-father, in his human understanding he learnt to discern the Father's will and to prepare himself to give his life as a ransom for the salvation of all whom he came to redeem (Cf Mt 20:28; 1 Tim 2:6).

In his public life, as the Gospels tell us, to do the Father's will was at the heart of Jesus's messianic mission. He said: *My food is to do the will of the one who sent me, and to complete his work* (Jn 4:34).

He taught his disciples to pray that the Father's will be done on earth as in heaven (Mt 6:10), and in the garden of Gethsemane, in agony, he declared himself to be ready to do the Father's will (Cf Mk 14:34-36).

St Paul prays for the Colossians that they may fully understand God's will for them (Col 1:9), and he encourages the faithful in Rome that through the renewal of their lives they should be able to discern God's will (Rom 12:2).

It is significant that in her messages at Medjugorje, Our Lady often urges us to deep prayer, the prayer of the heart, in order to discern the will of God, to understand his plan for us and through us:

Dear Children, I want you to understand that God has chosen each one of you, in order to use you in his great plan for the salvation of mankind. You cannot understand how great your role is in God's plan. Therefore, dear children, pray that in prayer you may comprehend God's plan through you (25 January 1987).

Dear Children, I call you to pray with the heart. You know that without prayer you cannot understand all that God is planning through each one of you. Therefore, pray! I wish that through each one of you God's plan may be fulfilled, and that everything which God has planted in your hearts may keep on growing. (25 April 1987).

In their prayerful conversation and reflection on the Scripture passages concerning the Messiah, Mary and Joseph must have gone through spiritual agony many times when thinking of those passages which foretold the sufferings of the Redeemer (e.g. Is 53, Ps 22). Joseph may have deeply worried over the prospect of his Son being the suffering servant of the Lord, the 'man of sorrows', the 'lamb led to the slaughter-house' (Is 53). He could not survive such a traumatic experience. I am sure, God in his mercy spared Joseph witnessing the terrible death of his Son, and that is why he passed away in the love and peace of the Holy Family.

Mary, on the other hand, was to remain at the side of Jesus in his hour of death. In the intervening years, not only Jesus was preparing himself for his messianic mission, but he had to help his Mother, too, to be prepared for her mission.

Mary preparing to become the Mother of Sorrows

The time between the death of Joseph and Jesus leaving home must have been a very difficult period of time for Mary, because she knew that the day would come when she would be all alone. Whatever happened to Jesus, it would affect her very much. Thinking much of Simeon's prophecy and of the various Scripture passages about the suffering Servant of God, Mary started seriously to experience the 'sword piercing her soul'.

Jesus may have noticed more than once that his Mother was quietly weeping and he may have asked her why she was crying. Mary would have told him about her worries concerning the future mission of Jesus and about the mysterious accounts of the prophets about the Lord's anointed servant, the Messiah. Sometimes they tell about the Messiah as the Shepherd King who will lead God's people on the path of peace and well-being, who will bring good news to the afflicted, heal the sick and free the captives:

The Lord Yahweh says this: 'Look, I myself shall take care of my flock and look after it. As a shepherd looks after his flock when he is with his scattered sheep, so shall I look after my sheep. I shall rescue them from wherever they have been scattered on the day of the clouds and darkness. I shall bring them back from the peoples where they are; I shall gather them back from the countries and bring them to their own land... I shall look for the lost one, bring back the stray, bandage the injured and make the sick strong. I shall watch over the fat and healthy. I shall be a true shepherd to them... I shall raise up one shepherd, my servant David, and put him in charge of them to pasture them; he will pasture them and be their shepherd... (Ezek 34:11-16, 23-31; Cf Jn 10).*

The spirit of the Lord is on me, for he has anointed me. He has sent me to bring the good news to the afflicted, to soothe the broken-hearted, to proclaim liberty to captives, release to those in prison, to proclaim a year of favour from the Lord... (Is 61:1-2; Cf Lk 4:16-21).

At other times, the prophets speak of the Messiah as an agent of God's retribution against the evil doers and will bring judgement on the enemies of God on the 'Day of the Lord':

The great Day of the Lord is near, and coming with great speed. How bitter the sound of the Day of the Lord, the Day when the warrior shouts his cry of war. That Day is a day of retribution, a day of distress and tribulation, a day of ruin and of devastation, a day of darkness and gloom...I shall bring such distress on humanity that they will grope their way like the blind for having sinned against the Lord...(Zeph 1:14-18; Amos 5:18-20; Cf Mt 3:7-12).

Mary may have mentioned also that many people were expecting a Messiah who would liberate Israel from the Romans. What most worrying for her, however, was that the prophets spoke also of the sufferings and cruel death of the Messiah. The Prophet Isaiah described the redeeming passion of God's servant in great detail about which Mary and Jesus may have reflected with deep emotions:

He was despised, the lowest of men, a man of sorrows, familiar with suffering, one from whom, as it were, we averted our gaze, despised, for whom we had no regard. Yet ours were the sufferings he was bearing, ours the sorrows he was carrying, while we thought of him as someone being punished and struck with affliction by God; whereas he was being wounded for our rebellions, crushed because of our guilt; the punishment reconciling us fell on him, and we have been healed by his bruises... Ill-treated and afflicted, he never opened his mouth, like a lamb led to the slaughter-house, like a sheep dumb before its shearers he never opened his mouth... It was the

Lord's good pleasure to crush him with pain, if he gives life as a sin offering, he will see his offspring and prolong his life, and through him the Lord's good pleasure will be done. After the ordeal he has endured, he will see the light and be content. By his knowledge, the upright one, my servant will justify many by taking their guilt on himself... (Is 53).

Mary may have thought also of the psalms which give cruel details of the Messiah's sufferings (Ps 22; 34:20; 69:21). The thought of her Son suffering like that made her to shed many tears. Mary may have recalled the words of the angel at the annunciation which convey a different image of the Messiah: *He will be great and will be called Son of the Most High. The Lord God will give him the throne of his ancestor David; he will rule over the House of Jacob forever and his reign will have no end* (Lk 1:32-33). It must have been a great mystery for Mary why the Son of God, the King of Kings, should suffer and die.

Holy Scripture must be fulfilled

We can assume that Jesus may have tried to comfort his Mother many times and as the years went by they talked and prayed much about the prophecies concerning the Messiah and his mission, especially his redeeming passion and death. As Jesus grew to adulthood and increased in wisdom, through deep prayer and with the help of his Mother, he learnt to understand more and more the Scripture passages about the Messiah, and in turn he was able to help his Mother to understand God's holy will about the way the Messiah had to fulfil his mission. He may have explained to her the meaning of the various images of the Messiah as given in Holy Scripture.

Perhaps Jesus recalled the words of the angel to his foster-father, Joseph, about the task his adopted Son will face: *He is the one who is to save his people from their sins* (Mt 1:21). So, the Messiah will not be a political liberator. He is sent to liberate the people of God and all people of the world from the power of Satan, reconciling them to the Father in Heaven, restoring God's reign in all hearts. Jesus explained to his Mother the way to achieve God's peace in all hearts. The Messiah had to show first the Father's love for his people by forgiving their sins, by healing the sick, by helping the downtrodden and by proclaiming the good news of God's kingdom everywhere, as foretold by the Prophet Isaiah (61:1-2; Lk 4:18-19).

Jesus must have shared with his Mother his understanding about his future task that he must become the Good Shepherd indeed who will look for the lost sheep, revealing God's love towards the sinner (Cf Jn 10; Lk 15).

It must have been most difficult for Jesus, however, to explain to his Mother why the Messiah had to suffer and die. He may have recalled the words of old Simeon, as told by Mary herself to Jesus, that he would be rejected by the people (Lk 2:34), because they were expecting a different Messiah. The Son of God becomes the 'man of sorrows', the Lamb of God, a lamb for sacrifice as Isaiah foretold (53:7), to 'expiate the sins of humanity' (Cf 1 Jn 4:10), to 'give his life as a ransom for many' (Mk 10:45; 1 Tim 2:5). Jesus may have raised Mary's spirit when he told her that she was to share his suffering in a special way as the 'Mother of Sorrows' and her participation in the work of redemption will be very important. Mary must have said in her heart many times the words: *I am the Lord's servant, let it happen to me as you have said* (Cf Lk 1:38).

Jesus spent much time in deep prayer, in union with his Father in Heaven, to comprehend fully, in his human understanding, God's holy will for his messianic mission, as foretold in Holy Scripture, and he was able to share with his Mother his own confidence and trust in God's goodness, especially when Jesus spoke to her about the glorious outcome of his redeeming work. The mission of the Messiah will not end by his death, because, as Scripture says, he will rise again to a glorious and eternal life. Mary will find his Son after three days, as she found him in the Temple after three days. The Father in Heaven would not allow his 'Holy One' to suffer corruption (Psalms 16:8-11; 49:15) and after his resurrection he will ascend to Heaven to sit and rule at the right hand of God (Ps 110:1; Cf Acts 2:24-36).

Jesus may have explained to his Mother also the third image of the Messiah as the Lord and Judge who is to punish the evil-doers, as foretold by Holy Scripture (Zeph 1:14-18; Amos 5:18-20; Dan 7:13-14). This will happen indeed on the 'Day of the Lord', when the Son of God comes again to judge the living and the dead, to achieve the final victory of God over the Evil One (Cf Mt 25:31-46). Yes, the prophets are right, but people fail to understand God's message because they seek their own desires and not the will of God.

Leaving home

During the last few years, before leaving home in Nazareth, Jesus must have shared many of his thoughts with his Mother to help her to be prepared for the greatest test any mother could have ever faced. It was not just about preparing for the final hour of agony on Calvary hill, but also about facing people who will turn against Jesus during his public life, accusingly pointing their finger at her, often abusing her as well. I do not think we ever can realize how much sorrow our Blessed

Mother had to live through. However, with the help and assuring love of Jesus, she must have felt confident to face the future whatever it might bring. Her trust in the goodness of God, in spite of all the wickedness of the world surrounding her, must have greatly increased through the comforting words of her Son and by seeing his great trust in his heavenly Father.

In turn, she must have assured Jesus not to worry about leaving her behind alone. She would be able to give some help here and there, and there were her relations and good neighbours who will help her in turn. Jesus should not feel worried about her, even if some people criticized him for letting his Mother live by herself. I mention these points, because one should be open to see the relationship of Jesus and Mary in the real human setting as well.

One day word came that John the Baptist was preaching and calling people to repentance at various parts of the river Jordan. Great crowds flocked to hear him and to be baptised by him. This was the signal for Jesus to wind up his job as carpenter and to get ready to start his own mission. His first act was to identify himself with the sinful humanity that he wanted to save. That is why his first steps took him to John the Baptist to be baptised by him who in turn would testify to him, pointing him out as the 'Lamb of God who takes away the sin of the world', and thus he was recruiting the first followers and disciples for Jesus (Cf Jn 1:29-51).

Before leaving home, I assume that Jesus and Mary had a very intimate conversation as to Mary's role in the future. For the time being, during his public ministry, Mary has to be in the background. In prayer and love they will always be united, very close to each other. But Mary's hour comes when the hour of Jesus arrives. Then will her special mission begin.

As tradition tells us, the apostle and evangelist John took care of Mary and she must have shared many of her experiences with John. I am sure that his Gospel was inspired by Our Lady. It is significant that John writes about the presence of Mary only twice, at the most important moments of Christ's mission, each time the 'hour of Jesus' was mentioned.

At the beginning, at the wedding of Cana (Jn 2:1-11), through Mary's intercession, Jesus performed his first miracle, inaugurating the Eucharistic mystery by changing water into wine, thus 'revealing his glory and his disciples believed in him'. But he also said to Mary, *My hour has not come yet*, implying that Mary's special role was not given until the 'final hour of Jesus' when he was dying. For John, the whole Eucharistic mystery and the mystery of Calvary are one. That is why he introduces his account of the Last Supper story with reference to the 'hour of Jesus':

Before the festival of the Passover, Jesus, knowing that his hour had come to pass from this world to the Father, having loved those who were his in the world, loved them to the end (Jn 13:1). Then, in the final hour, Mary's role is revealed: *Near the cross of Jesus stood his mother and his mother's sister, Mary the wife of Clopas, and Mary of Magdala. Seeing his mother and the disciple whom he loved standing near her, Jesus said to his mother, 'Woman, this is your son.' Then to the disciple he said, 'This is your mother.' And from **that hour** the disciple took her into his home* (Jn 19:25-27). It was in that hour that Mary became the New Eve, the Mother of the Church, the Mother of all God's children, helping them on their way to salvation. In their battle against the Evil One, Mary would be at their side and would 'crush the head of the serpent' (Cf Gen 3:15; Rev 12:17). *All generations will call her blessed, for the Almighty has done great things for her* (Lk 1:48).

Mary, the Mother and Teacher of Jesus, becomes the Mother and Teacher of his Body, the Church, as the second Vatican Council teaches: *The Son whom she brought forth is he whom God placed as the firstborn among many brethren (Cf Rom 8:29), namely the faithful, in whose birth and education she co-operates with a maternal love* (*Lumen Gentium*, No. 63).

Fatima and Medjugorje

It is significant that Our Lady, the Mother of the Church, has often responded to the prayer and faith of the Church in a special way.

In 1854 the Dogma of the Immaculate Conception was declared by Pope Pius IX, and four years later, on 11 February 1858, Our Lady appeared to St Bernadette at Lourdes, calling for repentance and naming herself, *'I am the Immaculate Conception.'* At the dawn of a secular and revolutionary age of conflicts and doubts, the Mother of the Church comes to the aid of her children and draws them to the fountain of healing through faith, especially to the Eucharist.

The parish priest at Knock in Ireland, Archdeacon Cavanagh, had a great devotion to the Holy Souls in Purgatory and in 1879 he offered one hundred Masses for them, commencing on 13th May. After completing this most remarkable act of charity, next day, on 21 August 1879, a heavenly tableau appeared against the end wall of the parish church. On the right was an altar with the lamb and cross, surrounded by adoring angels. On the left were three figures – Our Lady, wearing a crown, holding her hands high in a posture of prayer, with St Joseph on her right, and St John the evangelist on her left. This vision was seen by many villagers who gave evidence to the diocesan commissions later on. Through this vision, Our Lady, responding to the great faith of Father Cavanagh, wanted to bring not only comfort and consolation to the very poor and suffering people of that district, but, above all, she wanted to indicate the greatness and the immense efficacy of the sacrifice of the Holy Mass offered for the salvation of souls.

In 1895, 1897 and 1898 Pope Leo XIII wrote three Encyclical letters on the Holy Rosary, urging the faithful to take up the devotion of the Holy Rosary, reflecting on the mysteries of our redemption, for a threefold purpose: for the unity between the Churches of East and West; for the development of spiritual life in the faithful; to combat the evils of modern society and the threats of godless political movements. Twenty years later the Blessed Virgin Mary appeared in Fatima on 13 May 1917 to three children, introducing herself as the Queen of the Rosary, and asked them to make sacrifices and to pray the Rosary for peace, for ending the war, and for the conversion of sinners. She entered into the life of the Church and the world in a special way, with the mother's concern for the welfare of her children at the beginning of a century which was to bring untold sufferings and misery to millions of God's children. By means of the Holy Rosary and through consecration to her Immaculate Heart she offered her maternal mediation for the salvation of mankind, in response to the Church's faith in her powerful intercession.

We should not be surprised, therefore, that in the wake of the Second Vatican Council's teaching on her role in the life of the Church, Our Lady has responded as the Mother, Teacher and Model of the Church through her apparitions at Medjugorje, beginning on 24 June 1981. She calls herself the Queen of Peace, at a time when grave dangers are threatening the Church and the world; she renews the teaching of the Gospel about how to live in peace with God and with each other. Shortly after the outbreak of the war in former Yugoslavia, Our Lady at Medjugorje indicated that her concern for the Church and the world, expressed in Fatima, is continuing through her presence and messages at Medjugorje:

Dear Children, today I call you to pray as never before, now that my plan has begun to be realised. Satan is powerful and wants to sweep away the plans of peace and joy... For this reason, I urge you, dear children, that you pray and fast still more firmly. I am calling you to renunciation for nine days, so that, with your help, all that I wanted to realise through the secrets which I began at Fatima, may be fulfilled. I ask you, dear children, to grasp the importance of my coming and the gravity of the situation. I want to save all souls and present them to God. Therefore, let us pray that everything I have begun, be fully realised. Thank you for having responded to my call (25 August 1991).

One month later, in the context of the terrible war raging in former Yugoslavia, Our Lady urged us to help her Immaculate Heart to triumph over the power of the Evil One, as she asked the children of Fatima at the time of the First World War:

Dear Children, my special call today is to invite you all to prayer and self-denial, for now – as never before – Satan wants to show the world his shameful face by which he wants to seduce as many people as possible on the way of death and sin. Therefore, dear children, help my Immaculate Heart to triumph in a sinful world. I beseech all of you to offer prayers and sacrifices for my intentions, so that I can present them to God for what is most necessary. Forget your own desires, dear children, and pray for what God desires instead. Thank you for having responded to my call (25 September 1991).

Through Medjugorje, Our Lady has renewed her vitally important call to consecrate ourselves to the Sacred Heart of Jesus and to her Immaculate Heart, so that we may be able to overcome the evils of our troubled world:

Dear Children, my call to you to live the messages which I am giving you is a daily one, my special desire being, my dear children, to draw you closer to the Heart of Jesus. Therefore, dear children, I am calling you today to the prayer of consecration to Jesus, my dear Son, so that

*each of your hearts may be his. And then I am
calling you to consecration to my Immaculate
Heart. I want you to consecrate yourselves as
persons, families and parishes so that all belong
to God through my hands. Therefore, my dear
children, pray that you may comprehend the
greatness of this message which I am giving you.
I do not want anything for myself but all for the
salvation of your souls. Satan is powerful. For
this reason, my dear children, entrust yourselves,
by unceasing prayer, to my maternal heart. Thank
you for having responded to my call* (25 October
1988).

VII

Mary,
the Teacher of the Church

The title for this closing chapter is taken from the book of the late Cardinal Hans Urs von Balthasar, *Mary for Today* (*See* Introduction), although it follows also from the teaching of the Second Vatican Council on Our Lady's role in the life of the Church (Cf *Lumen Gentium*, No. 63). The basis for her role as Teacher of the Church is Christ's will in entrusting the Church in the person of St John to the spiritual motherhood of the Blessed Virgin Mary (Jn 19:5-27). This is how Pope Paul VI has interpreted the teaching of the Second Vatican Council on the spiritual motherhood of Mary in his Apostolic Exhortation *Marialis Cultus*, and Pope John Paul II in his Encyclical Letter *Redemptoris Mater* (*See* Introduction). We should, therefore, not be surprised, if the Mother of the Church fulfils her Christ-given role in the life of the Church in our time.

Our Lady fulfils her teaching role in a unique way through her special presence and messages at Medjugorje. I submit myself, of course, to the final decision of the Church regarding Medjugorje, but in the meantime, through these reflections, I am sharing my belief with the reader. In the Introduction to my reflections about Our Lady's teaching role I stated my belief that through her apparitions and messages at Medjugorje Our Lady established a school of prayer and love, a kind of 'Spiritual Nazareth' for our time. Her messages are the messages of the Gospel, expressed in the language of a mother. Her teaching role could be summed up in the words she spoke to the servants at the wedding of Cana: *Do whatever my Son tells you* (Jn 2:5). Her main objective is to mould us into the likeness of her Son, Jesus, so that we may become fitting instruments in God's plan for the salvation of mankind, as she told us in her first monthly message on 25 January 1987:

Dear Children, once again, I am calling you to start living a new life as from today. Dear children, I want you to understand that God has chosen each one of you, in order to use you in his great plan for the salvation of mankind. You cannot understand how great your role is in God's plan. Therefore, dear children, pray that in prayer you may comprehend God's plan through you. I am with you so that you may be able to bring it about in all its fullness. Thank you for having responded to my call.

As we approach the 2000th anniversary of the birth of Jesus of Nazareth, we have to look at Mary of Nazareth, the Mother and Teacher of

Jesus, who became the Mother and Teacher of his Body, the Church. It is significant that one of the visionaries in Medjugorje, Vicka, has received from Our Lady the story of her life in Nazareth. One day it will be published. We are looking forward with great eagerness to reading about the hidden life of Jesus, Mary and Joseph at Nazareth from the lips of Our Blessed Mother.

It is equally significant that the Holy Father, Pope John Paul II, in his *Bull of Indiction of the Great Jubilee of the year 2000, Incarnationis Mysterium*, dated 29 November 1998, in the final paragraph, puts before us the Mother of the Church who showed to everyone the way that leads to her Son, as our model, protectress and advocate:

The joy of the Jubilee would not be complete if our gaze did not turn to her who in full obedience to the Father gave birth to the Son of God in the flesh for our sake. For Mary 'the time to give birth' came to pass in Bethlehem (Lk 2:6), and filled with the Spirit she brought forth the First-Born of the new creation. Called to be the Mother of God, from the day of the virginal conception Mary lived the fullness of her motherhood, crowning it on Calvary at the foot of the Cross. There, by the wondrous gift of Christ, she also became the Mother of the Church, and showed to everyone the way that leads to her Son.

Woman of silence, given to listening, docile in the hands of the Father, the Virgin Mary is invoked as 'blessed' by all generations, for she recognized the marvels accomplished in her by the Holy Spirit. The nations will never grow weary of invoking the Mother of mercy and will always find refuge under her protection. May she who with Jesus her Son and Joseph her spouse went on pilgrimage to the holy Temple of God, guard the steps of all those who will be pilgrims in this Jubilee Year. And through the coming months may she deign to intercede intensely for the Christian people, so that abundant grace and mercy may be theirs, as they rejoice at the two thousand years since the birth of their Saviour.

One of the principal hopes of Pope John Paul II through the celebration of the Great Jubilee of the year 2000 is the meeting of all Christians, paving the way to final reconciliation and unity, expressed in his Apostolic Letter *Tertio Millennio Adveniente*:

The ecumenical and universal character of the Sacred Jubilee can be fittingly reflected by a meeting of all Christians. This would be an event of great significance, and so, in order to avoid misunderstandings, it should be properly presented and carefully prepared, in an attitude of fraternal cooperation with Christians of other denominations and traditions, as well as of grateful openness to those religions whose representatives might wish to acknowledge the joy shared by all the disciples of Christ (No. 55).

One of the main stumbling blocks to unity in Western Christianity is the place and role of the Blessed Virgin Mary in the Christian Church. As all Christians contemplate the mystery of the Incarnation in preparation for the Great Jubilee, let us hope that by reflecting on the Blessed Virgin Mary as the Teacher of Jesus, the humanity of Christ will be even more appreciated by Christians drawn closer to each other, recognising that *there is only one mediator between God and humanity, himself a human being, Christ Jesus, who offered himself as a ransom for all* (1 Tim 2:5).

At the same time, it is hoped that more and more Christians will recognise the vital role of the Blessed Virgin Mary, through her maternal mediation, in the realm of salvation. God has chosen human motherhood as a means for entering into our world, assuming our nature, born of a woman (Cf Gal 4:4-5), being nursed, taught and brought up by her, to be one of us: *It was essential that he should in this way be made completely like his brothers so that he could become a compassionate and trustworthy high priest for their relationship to God, able to expiate the sins of the people. For the suffering he himself passed through while being put to the test enables him to help others when they are being put to the test* (Heb 2:17-18).

Medjugorje, a Spiritual Nazareth

My first visit to Medjugorje was in May 1984. I was drawn there not so much by the reported daily apparitions of Our Lady to six teenagers since 24 June 1981, and by various phenomena there, but rather by what I had heard about the wonderful transformation in the lives of people there, in a then Communist country, in response to Our Lady's visitation. Ever since my first visit, my main interest has been to study the messages of Our Lady. In the course of these studies I discovered that the messages, given in the course of eighteen years, are not repetitive and random messages as many people may think. Many antagonists of Medjugorje focus their attention on superficial aspects and secondary phenomena of Medjugorje, or on the diocesan conflicts there, and thus they fail to recognise Our Lady's mission for our time: her teaching on Christian living in our troubled times, living the Gospel of Jesus and bearing witness to Jesus.

Our Lady gave us a blue-print for our striving for holiness by living a life of prayer and love, especially through her *Thursday Messages*, given through Marija Pavlovic, from 1 March 1984 to 8 January 1987, for the renewal of the parish of Medjugorje, to make the parish an example and model for the renewal of the whole Church. I published a handbook of spiritual exercises in

1991, *Living the Gospel with Our Lady*, based on Our Lady's *Thursday Messages* and corresponding Scripture texts.

The realisation in the course of 1987 that Our Lady's *Thursday Messages* covered exactly 150 weeks, suggested to me that perhaps the weeks could be divided into phases of ten weeks each, following the fifteen decades of the Rosary. To my surprise I found that each phase of ten weeks centred on a general theme, one leading to the next in a systematic way, giving a comprehensive three-year programme for the renewal of a parish, or of the whole Church. I summarize here Our Lady's teaching on the life of prayer and love.

First Year:
Invitation to the life of prayer and love
Our Lady's call:
1. To conversion, repentance, reparation and adoration of the Blessed Sacrament.
2. To open our hearts to the Holy Spirit.
3. To be prepared for spiritual warfare against Satan.
4. To shared prayer, in the family and community.
5. To love in the midst of adversities.

Second Year:

Growing in the life of prayer and love

Our Lady's call:

1. To make progress in the life of prayer and love.
2. To open our hearts to God through the prayer of the heart.
3. To use the various ways and means of Our Lady's protection against Satan.
4. To lead a life of holiness, goodness, obedience and love of God.
5. To abandon ourselves to God.

Third Year:

Transformation through the life of prayer and love

1. Conversion – change of heart is God's work.
2. Transformation is God's gift through Mary.
3. Fruits of Marian holiness of life.
4. The power of Marian holiness of life.
5. The glory of Marian holiness of life.

Another group of messages, the *Monthly Messages*, given by Our Lady through Marija Pavlovic on the 25th day of each month, since January 1987 to our present days, are addressed not only to the parish of Medjugorje, but to all the faithful who want to live by her messages. I found that these messages too follow a certain plan of spiritual formation, expanding the *Thursday Messages*, building up the whole spectrum of Christian living with evangelizing dimension to it, since Our Lady's main mission through Medjugorje is to rally her children to become instruments in her plan for the salvation of the world, as she told us in a monthly message on 25 March 1994:

Dear Children, today I rejoice with you and I call upon you to open yourselves to me and become instruments in my hands for the salvation of the world. I wish, my dear children, that all of you who have experienced the fragrance of holiness through these messages that I am giving you, would take it into this world which is hungry for God and for his love. I thank you all that you have responded in such large numbers and I bless you with my motherly blessing. Thank you for having responded to my call.

Our Lady's *Monthly Messages* are grouped on a yearly basis, centred on various aspects of Christian living. In due time my reflections on Our Lady's *Monthly Messages* will be published showing that Our Blessed Mother is the Teacher of the Church indeed. Here is a summary of the *Monthly Messages*, with a general theme for each year.

1987: New life in Christ.

1988: Growing in the divine life with Our Lady's help.

1989: The marks of holiness of life.

1990: Life of holiness under the protection of Our Lady.

1991: Called to become channels of God's peace.

1992: Renewal of our spiritual life with Our Lady's help.

1993: Building a new world of peace with Our Lady.

1994: Called to become instruments in Our Lady's hands for the salvation of the world.

1995: Our Lady leads us to the peace of Jesus, the King of Peace.

Through her messages since Christmas 1995, Our Lady is training us to become channels of God's peace for the reconciliation of the whole world, by deepening our life of prayer and love. These messages are in tune with the spirit of the Holy Father's guidance during these preparatory years leading up the Great Jubilee of the year 2000.

1996: Called to daily conversion and change to become a reflection of Jesus.

1997: Called to live the holiness of Christ by a deeper life of prayer and love.

1998: Called to live the holiness of Christ with the help of the Holy Spirit.

Epilogue

My main hope was and is to encourage the reader to have interest in further studies on the subjects I raised in my booklet and to allow his or her heart to open to God's inspiration to understand and appreciate more and more the wonderful mystery of the Incarnation and Our Lady's role in the life of a Christian.

If I may mention any particular point or points which have motivated me in my reflection on Our Lady's role in the life of Jesus and of his Body, the Church, as Mother, Teacher and Model, were these:

First, the many references in the Gospels to the prayer life of Jesus. These together with Our Lady's teaching at Medjugorje on prayer convinced me of the most vital importance of prayer in the life of a Christian, not just any prayer, but the unceasing prayer, the prayer of the heart which enables us to encounter God in the depth of our soul.

Secondly, Our Lady's role as Mother, Teacher and Model has a special message in our age for the role of parents, especially of mothers, many of whom fail to teach and guide their children in the ways of God. I hope and pray that the role of our Blessed Mother Mary as Teacher and Model will become an inspiration to all parents and to all of us.

Notes

1. *Mary Coredemptrix, Mediatrix, Advocate – Theological Foundations* – Towards a Papal Definition? Edited by Mark Miravalle STD. Published by Queenship Publishing, Santa Barbara, California.

2. Arius (c. 250 – c. 336), a Libyan by birth, was ordained priest during the reign of Pope Achillas (312-313) and put in charge of Baucalis, one of the principal churches at Alexandria. He came forward as a champion of subordinationist teaching about the Person of Christ and his views quickly spread under the heretical movement called Arianism which denied the true Divinity of Christ. Arianism maintained that the Son of God was not eternal but created by the Father from nothing as an instrument for the creation of the world; and that therefore he was not God by nature, but a changeable creature, his dignity as Son of God having been bestowed on him by the Father on account of his foreseen abiding righteousness. Arius and Arianism were condemned by the Council of Nicea (325). Cf *The Oxford Dictionary of the Christian Church*. Edited by F.L. Cross and E.A. Livingstone. Oxford University Press 1974. pp. 83, 87.

3. Nestorius (d. c. 451) and his heretic doctrine with the name Nestorianism taught that there were two separate Persons in the Incarnate Christ, the one Divine, and the other Human. Nestorius, a native of Germanicia in Syria Euphratensis, became Bishop of Constantinople in 428. The Council of Ephesus (431) condemned his doctrine. Cf *The Oxford Dictionary of the Christian Church*, pp. 961-963.

4. Monophysitism (from Greek *monos* = one, and *physis* = nature), a 5th century heresy, taught that in the Person of the Incarnate Christ there was but a single, and that a Divine, nature, as against the orthodox teaching of a double nature, Divine and Human, after the Incarnation.

The Dyophysite (two natures) doctrine was defined by the Council of Calcedon (451). Cf *The Oxford Dictionary of the Christian Church*, pp. 931-932.

5. *The Gospel of Jesus Christ* by Marie Joseph Lagrange OP. Published by Burns Oates & Washbourne Ltd., London 1938. First chapter: The Gospel of the Divine and human origin of Jesus. Jesus in his Father's house, Lk 2:40-52. p. 50.

6. *Mary the Mother of Jesus* by Dr Franz Michel Willam. Herder Book Co., St Louis, MO and London, 1954. Mary the Spiritual Guide of the Boy Jesus. Pp. 140-142.

7. *Encyclopedia of Theology*. Edited by Karl Rahner SJ Burns and Oates, 1981.

8. *Encyclopedia of Theology*. Jesus Christ – Problems and New Questions, pp.769-770. Grateful thanks to Canon Edward M. Stewart, STL, MA, of St Mary Immaculate Church of Warwick for his great help in rendering Rahner's text more readable. The actual text is as follows:

"*Jesus Christ's knowledge and freedom in his human reality.* An undefined doctrine of the Church attributes the direct vision of God to Jesus' human soul from the beginning of its existence. We can understand this thesis on the basis of the fundamental ontological condition which necessarily belongs to Jesus' human reality. For since being and consciousness are correlative, the ontic union of his humanity with God inevitably entails such an immediate relation to God. Even leaving out of account the fact this direct vision of God must not simply be identified with the beatific vision of the risen Christ, such a fundamental and in a certain sense 'transcendental' condition (existence on the basis of a most radical and unique link with God) does not entail that it must always have been explicitly reflected upon in all its implications and conceptually objectified. That would be simply incompatible with an honest exegesis of Lk 2:52; Mk 13:32; Mt 16:28. Nor does it mean that this fundamental condition, which is always the basis on which Jesus speaks, can be explicitly reflected upon, conceptually objectified and translated into language, except in contact with his historical experience, with the terms and concepts of his environment, and so with the human openness of his history. On that basis it is not impossible to assume a development in this 'translation' of his fundamental condition, which may even still be recognizable in the Synoptics."

9. Sources for the sections on the Sabbath, holy years and festivals: *Judaism* by Michael Kaniel, Blandford Press, Poole, Dorset, 1979; *Judaism: Practice and Belief, 63 BCE – 66 CE* by E.P. Sanders, Published by SCM Press, London, 1992; *A Feast in Honour of Jahweh* by Thierry Maertens, OSB, Published by Geoffry Chapman, London, 1966.

10. *To the Priests, Our Lady's Beloved Sons*, published by the Marian Movement of Priests, 11th English Edition. No. 330 (8 August 1986).